"This is a timely message for our culture, and I cannot think of a better person to deliver it. Mark is an excellent expositor of God's Word, but in *Play the Man* he is showing us how to live it out. Challenging men to reject the status quo, Mark helps them refocus, rally, and do the work of revitalizing their homes, churches, and culture in general. This book will take you out of your comfort zone to reach your God-given calling. I am so proud that Mark took on this important and needed project."

—**Carey Casey**, National Center for Fathering

"You won't accomplish anything if don't play the game. You can't be MVP unless you finish the game. All this starts with a clear decision to 'play the man.' This book is full of personal, biblical, and historical stories that encourage, challenge, and teach you how to go from boy to man. How to go from being trained to training others or from a son to a father or, as I put it, a young warrior to a hero. Read this book and learn what it takes to be the man God created you to be. Here's the good news. You'll find out you already have what it takes. Let's go!"

—**Shaun Alexander**, award-winning author of *Touchdown Alexander* and *The Walk*, 2005 NFL MVP, and host of the radio/podcast show *Finish the Game*

"If there's one thing I've learned from reading Mark Batterson's work throughout the years, it's that he has the amazing ability to make the written word feel like a face-to-face conversation. In *Play the Man*, Mark is speaking to me right where I live at this very moment. Even more important, he's speaking to all men faced with the awesome responsibility of raising up the next generation. His ideas, advice, and encouragement are priceless."

—**Ernie Johnson Jr.**, TNT sportscaster and author of *Unscripted*

"My baseball off-season consists of rest, reading, and replenishing the reserve tank. A 162-game schedule on top of a two-month spring training is taxing on any man. I look to equip my heart and mind with encouraging words. I can imagine no better companion during this time than Mark Batterson. Mark is one of my favorite writers, and he hits a grand slam with *Play the Man*."

—**Steve Foster**, Colorado Rockies pitching coach

PLAY
THE
MAN

BECOMING
THE MAN
GOD CREATED
YOU TO BE

Mark Batterson

BakerBooks

a division of Baker Publishing Group
Grand Rapids, Michigan

Published by Baker Books
a division of Baker Publishing Group
P.O. Box 6287, Grand Rapids, MI 49516-6287
www.bakerbooks.com

Printed in the United States of America

Library of Congress Cataloging-in-Publication Data is on file at the Library of Congress, Washington, DC.

ISBN 978-0-8010-1898-5 (cloth)
ISBN 978-0-8010-7561-2 (ITPE)

Unless otherwise indicated, Scripture quotations are from the Holy Bible, New International Version®. NIV®. Copyright © 1973, 1978, 1984, 2011 by Biblica, Inc.™ Used by permission of Zondervan. All rights reserved worldwide. www.zondervan.com

Scripture quotations labeled AKJV are from the American King James Version, produced by Stone Engelbrite.

Scripture quotations labeled BSB are from The Holy Bible, Berean Study Bible, BSB, Copyright © 2016 by Bible Hub. All Rights Reserved Worldwide.

Scripture quotations labeled ESV are from The Holy Bible, English Standard Version® (ESV®), Copyright © 2001 by Crossway, a publishing ministry of Good News Publishers. Used by permission. All rights reserved. ESV Text Edition: 2011.

Scripture quotations labeled ISV are from the The Holy Bible: International Standard Version® Release 2.1. Copyright © 1995-2012. The ISV Foundation. All rights reserved internationally.

Scripture quotations labeled KJV are from the King James Version of the Bible.

Scripture quotations labeled KJV 2000 are from The King James 2000 Bible, copyright © Doctor of Theology Robert A. Couric 2000, 2003. Used by permission. All rights reserved.

Scripture quotations labeled NASB are from the New American Standard Bible®, copyright © 1960, 1962, 1963, 1968, 1971, 1972, 1973, 1975, 1977, 1995 by The Lockman Foundation. Used by permission. (www.Lockman.org)

Scripture quotations labeled NET are from the NET Bible®, copyright © 1996-2006 by Biblical Studies Press, L.L.C. http://netbible.com. Used by permission. All rights reserved.

Scripture quotations labeled NLT are from the *Holy Bible*, New Living Translation, copyright © 1996, 2004, 2015 by Tyndale House Foundation. Used by permission of Tyndale House Publishers, Inc., Carol Stream, Illinois 60188. All rights reserved.

Published in association with the literary agency of The Fedd Agency, Inc., Austin, Texas.

17 18 19 20 21 22 23   7 6 5 4 3 2 1

CONTENTS

INTRODUCTION

Let us play the men for our people.

—2 Samuel 10:12 KJV

February 23, AD 155[1]
Smyrna, Greece

Like a scene straight out of *Gladiator*, Polycarp was dragged into the Roman Colosseum. Discipled by the apostle John himself, the aged bishop faithfully and selflessly led the church at Smyrna through the persecution prophesied by his spiritual father. "Do not be afraid of what you are about to suffer," writes John in Revelation 2:10. "Be faithful, even to the point of death."

John had died a half century before, but his voice still echoed in Polycarp's ears as the Colosseum crowd chanted, "Let loose the lion!" That's when Polycarp heard a voice from heaven that was audible above the crowd:

"Be strong, Polycarp. Play the man."

Days before, Roman bounty hunters had tracked him down. Instead of fleeing, Polycarp fed them a meal. Perhaps that's why they granted his last request—an hour of prayer. Two hours later, many of those who heard the way Polycarp prayed actually repented of their sin on the spot. They did not, however, relent of their mission.

Like Jesus entering Jerusalem, Polycarp was led into the city of Smyrna on a donkey. The Roman proconsul implored Polycarp to recant. "Swear by the genius of Caesar!" Polycarp held his tongue, held his ground. The proconsul prodded, "Swear, and I will release thee; revile the Christ!"

"Eighty and six years have I served Him," said Polycarp. "And He has done me no wrong! How then can I blaspheme my King who saved me?"

The die was cast.

Polycarp was led to the center of the Colosseum where three times the proconsul announced, "Polycarp has confessed himself to be a Christian." The bloodthirsty crowd chanted for death by beast, but the proconsul opted for fire.

As his executioners seized his wrists to nail him to the stake, Polycarp stopped them. "He who gives me strength to endure the fire will enable me to do so without the help of your nails."

As the pyre was lit on fire, Polycarp prayed one last prayer: "I bless you because you have thought me worthy of this day and this hour to be numbered among your martyrs in the cup of your Christ."[2] Soon the flames engulfed him, but strangely they did not consume him. Like Shadrach, Meshach, and Abednego before him, Polycarp was fireproof. Instead of the stench of burning flesh, the scent of frankincense wafted through the Colosseum.[3]

Using a spear, the executioner stabbed Polycarp through the flames. Polycarp bled out, but not before the twelfth martyr of Smyrna had lived out John's exhortation: *be faithful even to the point of death*. Polycarp died fearlessly and faithfully. And the way he died forever changed the way those eyewitnesses lived. He did what the voice from heaven had commanded. Polycarp played the man.

Make Men of Them

In 1744, the College of William and Mary sent a letter to six Native American chiefs, offering a free education to twelve of their young braves.[4] The chiefs politely declined the offer with the following reply:

> Several of our young People were formerly brought up at the colleges of the Northern Provinces; they were instructed in all your sciences; but when they came back to us they were bad Runners, ignorant of every means of living in the Woods, unable to bear Cold or Hunger, knew neither how to build a cabin, take a Deer or kill an enemy, spoke our Language imperfectly, and were therefore neither fit for Hunters, Warriors, or Counselors; they were totally good for nothing.

The chiefs then made an offer of their own:

> If the Gentlemen of Virginia will send us a Dozen of their Sons, we will take care of their Education; instruct them in all we know, and make Men of them.[5]

I've taken more classes in more subjects than I can recall. I've been instructed in everything from ancient history to astrophysics, meteorology to immunology, psychology to pneumatology. But never once have I taken a class on manhood. That class wasn't offered—not even as an elective!

I fear we have forgotten how to make men.

I fear we have forgotten how to play the man.

Before we go any further, let me offer a disclaimer. In many ways, I feel like the least qualified man to write this book. Simply put, I lack man skills. If an assembly project requires more than two steps, it's not going to end well for me. My family affectionately calls me an "unhandy man." And to be honest, my version of roughing it involves an air-conditioned cabin with a fully stocked refrigerator.

I've had more than my fair share of adventures, such as hiking the Inca Trail to Machu Picchu. But in the spirit of full disclosure, I packed an inflatable mattress. When we set up camp the first night, a strange mechanical sound echoed throughout the campsite. That was me and my inflatable mattress motor! Did I feel a little less manly than the rest of the guys? Yes, yes I did. But I highly value sleep, and I slept great!

I might also add that I can change a flat tire, but I usually call AAA. And I did deep-fry a turkey once, emphasis on *deep-fry.*

You get the picture. I lack man skills, but that is *not* what playing the man is about.

You don't have to eat the heart of a bear or sleep inside a dead horse like Leonardo DiCaprio in *The Revenant.* That might win you some man points, or even an Oscar, but that isn't what playing the man is all about.

In the pages that follow, I'll unveil seven virtues of manhood—tough love, childlike wonder, will power, raw passion, true grit, clear vision, and moral courage. Just in case any women get their hands on this book, these virtues aren't exclusive to men, but I find men lack them more often than women, and in some respects, they are more important for men. The seven virtues are not an exhaustive list either, but they give us a starting block.

After exploring how to play the man, I'll switch gears and talk about how to make a man. I love youth pastors. I thank God for youth pastors. But it's not their job to disciple my children. That's my job! If you weren't discipled by your father, it can be tough to disciple your son because you don't know where to begin. I realize I'm only a data point of one, but I'll share the Discipleship Covenant I created for my sons and the Rite of Passage I took them through at the end of what we called the "Year of Discipleship." These things are not bulletproof or foolproof, but they are a starting point in the journey toward manhood. My goal is to give you a template you can adopt and adapt.

Now, let me paint a picture—the big picture.

Untamed

A decade ago I spent an unforgettable week in the Galapagos Islands. This archipelago of islands off the coast of Ecuador hasn't changed much since Charles Darwin sailed there on the HMS *Beagle* in December 1831 and studied fifteen species of finches. The Galapagos may be the closest thing to the Garden of Eden left on Earth!

My son and I saw a two-hundred-year-old turtle weighing in at nearly a thousand pounds. We came face-to-face with giant iguanas that weren't the least bit intimidated by humankind. We watched pelicans that looked like prehistoric pterodactyls dive into the ocean and come back up with breakfast in their oversized beaks. And we went swimming with sea lions, which we later learned isn't altogether safe!

A few weeks after returning home, our family went to the National Zoo in Washington, DC. The National Zoo is a great zoo, but zoos are ruined for me. Looking at caged animals isn't nearly as exhilarating as witnessing a wild animal in its natural habitat—it's too safe, it's too tame, and it's too predictable.

As we walked through the ape house, the four-hundred-pound gorillas looked so bored, so emasculated, behind protective plexiglass. That's when a thought fired across my synapses: *I wonder if churches do to people what zoos do to animals.*

I don't think it's intentional. In fact, it's well-intentioned. But I wonder if our attempts to *help* people sometimes *hurt* them. We try to remove the danger, remove the risk. We attempt to tame people in the name of Christ, forgetting that Jesus didn't die to keep us safe. Jesus died to make us dangerous.

> I am sending you out like sheep among wolves. Therefore be as shrewd as snakes and as innocent as doves.[6]

That doesn't sound safe, does it? That's because it's *not*. The will of God isn't an insurance plan. The will of God is a dangerous plan. It takes tons of testosterone, and it produces high levels of holy adrenaline.

Now, let me add a frame to the picture that Jesus painted.

Rewilding

In 1995, the gray wolf was reintroduced to Yellowstone National Park after a seventy-year hiatus. Scientists expected an ecological ripple effect, but the size and scope of the trophic cascade took them by surprise.[7]

Wolves are predators that kill certain species of animals, but they indirectly give life to others. When the wolves re-entered the ecological equation, it radically changed the behavioral patterns of other wildlife. As the wolves began killing coyotes, the rabbit and mouse populations increased, thereby attracting more hawks, weasels, foxes, and badgers.

In the absence of predators, deer had overpopulated the park and overgrazed parts of Yellowstone. Their new traffic patterns, however, allowed the flora and fauna to regenerate. The berries on those regenerated shrubs caused a spike in the bear population.

In six years' time, the trees in overgrazed parts of the park had quintupled in height. Bare valleys were reforested with aspen, willow, and cottonwood trees. And as soon as that happened, songbirds started nesting in the trees. Then beavers started chewing them down. Beavers are ecosystem engineers, building dams that create natural habitats for otters, muskrats, and ducks, as well as fish, reptiles, and amphibians.

One last ripple effect.

The wolves even changed the behavior of rivers—they meandered less because of less soil erosion. The channels narrowed and pools formed as the regenerated forests sta-bilized the riverbanks.

My point? We need wolves!

When you take the wolf out of the equation, there are unintended consequences. In the absence of danger, a sheep remains a sheep. And the same is true of men. The way we play the man is by overcoming overwhelming obstacles, by meeting daunting challenges. We may fear the wolf, but we also crave it. It's what we want. It's what we need.

Picture a cage fight between a sheep and a wolf. The sheep doesn't stand a chance, right? Unless there is a Shepherd. And I wonder if that's why we play it safe instead of playing the man—we don't trust the Shepherd.

Playing the man starts there!

Ecologists recently coined a wonderful new word. Invented in 2011, *rewilding* has a multiplicity of meanings. It's resisting the urge to control nature. It's the restoration of wilderness. It's the reintroduction of animals back into their natural habitat. It's an ecological term, but rewilding has spiritual implications.

As I look at the Gospels, rewilding seems to be a subplot. The Pharisees were so civilized—too civilized. Their religion was nothing more than a stage play. They were wolves in sheep's clothing.[8] But Jesus taught a very different brand of spirituality.

"Foxes have dens and birds have nests," said Jesus, "but the Son of Man has no place to lay his head."[9] So Jesus spent the better part of three years camping, fishing, and hiking with His disciples. It seems to me Jesus was rewilding them.

Jesus didn't just teach them how to be fishers of men.

Jesus taught them how to play the man!

That was my goal with the Year of Discipleship, which I'll outline in chapter 9. To celebrate the completion of the covenant, I took each of my sons on a Rite of Passage trip. Parker's trip was hiking the Grand Canyon from rim to rim. That 23.2-mile hike still ranks as one of the hardest things I've ever done, in part because of the July temperatures that hit 110 degrees—and that was in the shade! But I gained some life lessons that couldn't be learned any other way.

A man discovers who he is in the wild.

He also discovers who God is.

Even Jesus went off the grid for forty days. You have to put yourself in situations where everything is stripped away, where nothing is scripted. You have to put yourself at the mercy of the elements and test your limits. That's how you discover what you're capable of and, more important, what God is capable of. That's how boys become men and men become men of God.

This book is for the man who wants to play the man but isn't entirely sure how. It's for the man who wants to be a father his children can honor and a husband his wife can respect, but he needs a little help. And the simple fact that you've picked up this book tells me that's *you*.

The Enigma

There is an old axiom: "Men are from Mars and women are from Venus."[10] But since we both live on Earth, we better figure this thing out. What does it mean to play the man? The white noise of cultural confusion coupled with the deafening silence of the church has left us insecure and unsure of our manhood. So we settle for something far less than what God originally intended.

Male and female he created them.[11]

Gender was God's idea. So it's not just a good idea; it's a God idea. And that goes for sex too, by the way. Manhood isn't a subject to be avoided. It's an objective to be sought after and celebrated. But where do we start?

The answer is God's original intent, God's original design. We must examine the first Adam, Adam—he's the prototype. And we must cross-examine the second Adam, Jesus—He's the archetype.

When the compass needle of masculinity is spinning, Jesus is true north. First Adam helps us understand what went wrong. Second Adam helps us make it right.

In many respects, Jesus is a study in contrasts. He is the Lamb of God and the Lion of the Tribe of Judah. He is gentle Jesus, meek and mild. But meek isn't weak, and Jesus definitely had a wild side! He was tough as nails, seven-inch nails that pierced His hands and feet. But He was also man enough to cry.

Jesus is an enigma, the Enigma, and that is because He was fully God, fully man. Yes, He is the omniscient, omnipotent, and omnipresent Son of God. But for thirty-three years, Jesus played the man. He subjected Himself to the laws of nature He created, taking on flesh and blood. It almost sounds sacrilegious, but Jesus went through puberty just like we do. Like us, He had to learn reading, writing, and arithmetic. And He had to discover His destiny, His identity, and His masculinity. Of course, after discovering it, He defined it.

Manhood Virtues

In his brilliant book *The Road to Character*, David Brooks makes a distinction between résumé virtues and eulogy virtues. Résumé virtues are the skills you need to *make a living*, and those are often the most celebrated virtues in our culture. But when it comes to *making a life*, eulogy virtues win the day. These are the virtues that get talked about at your funeral.[12]

One danger of writing a book on manhood is that it's very difficult to decode the difference between biblical prototypes and cultural constructs. Much of what it means to be a man is determined by tradition. The expectations placed on men in first-century Israel and twenty-first-century America are very different. But I'll do my best to decipher the difference between the hardwiring—the image of God in us—and the software—cultural expectations.

It's increasingly difficult to differentiate culturally between what it means to be a man and what it means to be a woman. And for that very reason, it is more and more important to do so!

Every man needs a résumé, but that isn't the focus of this book. Man skills may win you man points, but manhood *virtues* win the heart of God. Virtue is much harder to develop than skill, and it takes much longer. But the payoff is far greater!

Don't beat yourself up if you fall short on any of these seven virtues. Remember, Jesus already paid the penalty for your sin. Don't try to double pay with feelings of guilt. Philippians 2:12 provides a good guideline for this:

Work out your salvation with fear and trembling.

The irony of this statement is that salvation cannot be earned by good works; it can only be received as a free gift. But once you receive the gift of salvation, you have to take it to the gym and work it out.

You exercise virtue the same way you exercise muscles. You have to push them to their limits until they literally tremble. That's how you know the muscle fiber is breaking down, and that's how it gets built back up even stronger!

This might be a good opportunity for me to recommend that you read this book with someone else. Why? Because iron sharpens iron! You need someone to push you, someone to spot you. I know men have a reputation for being as relational as inanimate objects, but you can't reach your full potential without a band of brothers.

One final challenge.

The twentieth president of the United States, James B. Garfield, served two hundred days in office before being gunned down. Garfield is the only president who was also an ordained minister. And Garfield is the only president who didn't run for president! The 1880 Republican National Convention was in a deadlock after the thirty-fifth ballot. Garfield wasn't even on the ballot at the beginning of the convention, but he somehow managed to win the nomination on the thirty-sixth ballot.

How did a man who didn't seek the presidency end up in the White House? I'm not a political scientist, but I have a theory. I think it traces back to a defining decision James Garfield made as a young man.

"I mean to make myself a man," said Garfield, "and if I succeed in that, I shall succeed in everything else."[13]

Garfield made himself a man.

Then America made him president.

I'm not giving you a formula for becoming the next president of the United States. I am, however, giving you a formula for greatness, no matter who you are or what you do.

Like me, you wear many different hats. And you have many different dreams, no doubt. But if you focus on playing the man, everything else will fall into place. If you succeed at that, you will succeed at everything else.

Play the man!

PART 1

PLAY THE MAN

THE SEVEN VIRTUES

1

Tough as Nails

The First Virtue of Manhood:
Tough Love

Behold, their brave men cry in the streets.

—Isaiah 33:7 NASB

May 20, 1927
Roosevelt Field, Long Island

At 7:52 a.m., a twenty-five-year-old pilot named Charles Lindbergh fired up his single-seat, single-engine airplane, the *Spirit of St. Louis*. Lindbergh almost ran out of runway before takeoff, but no brakes meant no turning back! Thirty-three hours, thirty minutes, and thirty seconds later, Lindbergh touched down in an airfield outside Paris, becoming the first person to make a solo nonstop transatlantic flight.

Half a dozen pilots before him had failed, buried at sea. And Lindbergh's flying résumé paled in comparison to theirs.

He was a mail pilot with a handful of barnstorming events under his belt. But what he lacked in experience, he more than made up for with mental toughness.

Lindbergh had no radio and no fuel gauge. He also got next to no sleep the night before! Because of weight limitations, Lindbergh hardly packed anything, not even a toothbrush. He only took one quart of water and five ham and chicken sandwiches. He ate only one of them.

Through the darkness of a moonless night, Lindbergh aimed at Europe. He flew as high as ten thousand feet and as low as ten feet, fighting thousands of miles of fog over the Atlantic Ocean. Lindbergh got the first hint that land was nearby when he saw a fishing boat as morning dawned on the second day. He closed the throttle and circled the boat, yelling, "Which way is Ireland?" The poor fisherman either didn't speak English or was too spooked to answer.[1]

As the sun set for the second time in his epic journey, the lights of Le Bourget paved the way to Paris. He circled the Eiffel Tower, then flew toward what he thought would be an empty airfield. He found the airfield all right, but it wasn't empty. Instead, a huge crowd crying, "*Vive!*" gave Lindbergh a hero's welcome. Lindbergh won not only the $25,000 Orteig Prize for the first nonstop flight from New York to Paris, but he also won the hearts of people around the world.

The day after his flight, newspapers ran 250,000 stories totaling thirty-six million words. One publication called it "the greatest event since the resurrection." Lindbergh received so much fan mail—3.5 million letters—that thirty-eight Western Union employees were assigned to manage his mail.

So how did Lindbergh do it? How did he succeed in doing something so many others had failed to do? How did he endure the fog, the fear, the fatigue?

Here's my theory.

During the darkest hours of the night, I bet Charles Lindbergh thought of his grandfather, August Lindbergh.

In 1859, August Lindbergh immigrated to America from Sweden and found work at a sawmill in Sauk Centre, Minnesota. Two years later, Lindbergh fell into a whirring saw blade that tore through his upper torso. It left such a gaping hole that one eyewitness said they could see his beating heart.[2]

A half-conscious Lindbergh was carried home, where he waited *three days* for a doctor! When the doctor finally reached Lindbergh, he amputated what was left of his arm and sewed up the hole. Now, here's the amazing thing: August Lindbergh didn't scream or cry. Not even an "ouch!" He toughed it out, suffering in silence.[3]

With a grandfather like that, is it any wonder Charles crossed the Atlantic? Compared to all the pain and agony that his grandfather endured, a solo flight across the Atlantic was a cakewalk.

Toughen Up

Next time someone complains a little too much about their aches and pains, tell them about August Lindbergh. I actually tried this with my youngest son, Josiah, when he was twelve years old. He might have been a tad too young for that gory story, but it worked like a charm. He quit complaining!

Reality check: most of our problems are first-world problems.

My wife, Lora, recently spent several days in a Syrian refugee camp on the border of Greece and Macedonia. The horrors that many of those refugees have endured is unconscionable—homes destroyed by bombs, families torn apart by civil war, children drowned at sea trying to escape. We have Syrian refugee friends who recently immigrated to the United States who actually buried their sixteen-year-old son alive for nine hours to protect him from being forcibly recruited to join ISIS. That will put your problems into perspective in a hurry.

The refugees can't go back home to Syria because their houses are destroyed, and they can't go forward because of a barbed-wire fence at the border. It's not unlike the situation the Israelite refugees found themselves in after the exodus—trapped between an uncrossable Red Sea and a stampeding Egyptian army.

That's a *tough spot*.

We, however, get frustrated when we miss a connecting flight or can't hook up to the internet. Really? We get upset over a thirty-minute delay before boarding a 450-ton Boeing 747 that will soar to thirty thousand feet in the air and get us wherever we want to go at half the speed of sound. We need to keep checking our perspective.

Sometimes we need to lighten up.

Sometimes we need to toughen up.

I'm not advocating wholesale stoicism. I am advocating a single virtue—toughness. It comes in lots of shapes and sizes, from physical toughness to mental toughness. But in this chapter I want to focus on the rarest form of toughness—tough love. That's the first virtue of manhood.

Tough love is far more difficult to attain than physical toughness, and far more important. It sets the men apart

24

from the boys! A tough guy isn't someone who can blacken an eye or bloody a nose; it's someone who is willing to be nailed to a cross for someone they love.

Playing the man is tough love!

Take Up Your Cross

When you hear the phrase "tough guy," who do you think of? Some people think of baseball iron man Cal Ripken or NFL icon Brett Favre. Or perhaps you recall your favorite film hero. Certainly William Wallace or Maximus Decimus Meridius come to mind for many! And they qualify as tough guys, no doubt.

But none of them carried a cross to Golgotha and then allowed themselves to be hammered to it with seven-inch nails.[4] And if we had been eyewitnesses to the crucifixion, we wouldn't read Luke 9:23 the same way:

> Whoever wants to be my disciple must deny themselves and take up their cross daily and follow me.

Take up your cross.

We say it so effortlessly, so flippantly. But that's because we read it figuratively. It's estimated that a Roman cross weighed three hundred pounds, and even if Jesus carried only the crossbar, it was still placed on raw flesh that had just been flogged! And He carried it no less than 650 yards down the *Via Dolorosa*.[5]

When I say "tough as nails," this is what I mean. It's the epitome of toughness. Being a *tough guy* doesn't mean sticking up for yourself when you get offended. A true *tough guy* sacrifices himself for the sake of others.

Jesus didn't just carry a three-hundred-pound cross; He carried the weight of the world. Every offense ever committed was placed on His shoulders, and He carried it all the way to Calvary.

Love Who?

In 1992, a grand dragon in the Ku Klux Klan made front-page news. For years, Larry Trapp terrorized a Jewish leader in his community named Michael Weisser, making death threats against him and his synagogue. Then one day Larry tore his Nazi flags, destroyed his hate literature, and renounced the KKK. Why? Because when Larry Trapp was dying of a diabetes-related kidney disease and unable to care for himself, Michael Weisser took him into his home and cared for him. "He showed me so much love," said Larry Trapp, "that I could not help but love [him] back."

That's tough love!

> Very rarely will anyone die for a righteous person, though for a good person someone might possibly dare to die. But God demonstrates his love for us in this: While we were still sinners, Christ died for us.[6]

Tough love is loving others when they least expect it and least deserve it.

The message of the gospel can be captured in two words: *love conquers*. But that love is not the puppy love our culture celebrates à la *The Bachelorette*. It's a long-suffering love. It's a love that always protects, always trusts, always hopes, always perseveres.[7] It's a love that even loves its enemies.

Tough love is sacrificial love—a love that is willing to be nailed to a cross for someone else's sin. Tough love is unconditional love—a love that is not dictated by someone else's performance. Tough love is covenantal love—for better or for worse, for richer or for poorer, in sickness and in health.

It's easy loving your wife when everything is going great, right? When it's not going great, it's not so easy. Why? Because our love tends to be *reactive*. Tough love is *proactive*. It's not a need-seeking love; it's a need-meeting love. It doesn't seek validation, because it doesn't need any! It adds value to the beloved!

One of the great mistakes we make is thinking that God feels about us the same way we feel about ourselves. So we project our imperfections onto God. The reality is this: *there is nothing you can do to make God love you any more or any less than He already does.* God loves you perfectly, eternally.

I know you know that, but do you believe it?

Simply put: you mean the cross to Christ.

When we are at our worst, God is at His best. Think of it as the sacrifice of love, and like the sacrifice of praise, it may be the most meaningful form of love because it means loving someone when you least feel like it.

Unbar the Doors

I recently spoke to a conference of pastors in Great Britain, and my speaking slot happened to be right after Justin Welby, the archbishop of Canterbury. Not an easy act to follow! I pastor a church that is twenty years old, and I can hardly believe it's been twenty years. Archbishop Welby pastors a church that dates all the way back to AD 509. He's the 105th archbishop in a lineage that traces to Augustine of Canterbury.

During his talk, Archbishop Welby shared a story about Thomas Becket, one of his predecessors, who was murdered in 1171. Archbishop Becket and King Henry II didn't get along so well. In fact, the king said something to the effect of, "Who will rid me of this troublesome priest?"[8] Four knights interpreted that question as a royal command and set out to confront the archbishop. Arriving on December 29, 1170, they hid their weapons under a tree outside Canterbury Cathedral and their armor under their cloaks. When Becket refused to go with them peaceably, the knights retrieved their swords. The archbishop's clerics told him to bar the doors of the cathedral, but Becket did the opposite. "Unbar the doors!" he shouted. "Unbar the doors!"[9]

This is rather gruesome, but the crown of Becket's head was cut off, his brains spilling out. Becket's blood dyed the floor of the cathedral a crimson red.

It's on the very spot where Becket's blood was spilled that his assassination is rehearsed every year with the presiding archbishop playing the role of Becket. It's a solemn ritual, a profound reminder that, in the words of Archbishop Welby: "What we believe is worth dying for."[10]

So let me ask you this: Is your version of Christianity worth dying for?

It was for Thomas Becket. It was for eleven of the twelve apostles who were mercilessly martyred for their faith. And it was for an eighty-six-year-old bishop named Polycarp who played the man.

How about you?

Anger Issues

In *Rocky III*, Rocky's rematch with Clubber Lang is a classic fight scene. Rocky takes it on the chin over and over and over, but he does it intentionally, mockingly. "You ain't so bad," he says, taunting Lang. "C'mon. You ain't so bad. You ain't so bad." His confused manager, Apollo Creed, calls it crazy: "He's getting killed!" Rocky's brother-in-law, Paulie, calls it strategy. "He's not getting killed, he's getting mad."[11]

We think of anger as being sinful, but sometimes not getting angry is sinful. The key is getting angry about the right thing, at the right time, in the right way. In the words of Aristotle, "Anybody can become angry, that is easy; but to be angry with the right person, and to the right degree, and at the right time, and for the right purpose, and in the right way, that is not within everybody's power, that is not easy."[12]

Anger is *not* sin. In fact, Scripture uses the strongest type of anger, *hate*, to describe how we should feel about sin.[13] And if we hated sin more, we might do it less! Now, if that gets translated the wrong way, it's extremely dangerous. It's *sin*, not *sinners*.

Jesus got mad.

He got mad at the hypocrisy of the Pharisees. He got mad at death when it robbed Him of His friend Lazarus. He got mad at the disciples when they tried to deter Him from the cross. He got mad at the money changers who turned the temple into a den of thieves, and then He threw a temple tantrum!

That's tough love!

Now, here's a little tip. If you try to play God instead of playing the man, it won't work out so well. When you try to do God's job for Him, it backfires. It's the Holy Spirit's job to convict; it's your job to love.

We all have anger issues. It's important that we ask ourselves, *What am I getting angry at?* Some of us beat ourselves up because of the mistakes we've made, but those self-inflicted wounds undermine what God is trying to do in us and through us. Sometimes we get mad at God, thinking He is responsible for something that has happened in our lives. If we're going to get mad, we should get mad at the one who kills, steals, and destroys.

Here's some homework: take an anger inventory.

When do you get angry? Why? And what is the outcome? Do an anger autopsy. That's how you identify your triggers. Nine times out of ten, the trigger is not getting what you want when you want it. Which brings us right back to selfishness. You have to identify your sin triggers so you can lock the trigger instead of pulling it.

Thou Shalt Offend Pharisees

"Who am I going to offend?"

That is one of the most important questions a man has to ask himself—and answer. This I promise you: you're going to offend someone! So who will it be? If you're afraid of offending people, you'll offend God. If you're afraid of offending God, you'll offend people. It's one or the other!

My advice? *Offend Pharisees!* That's what Jesus did, and He did it with great intentionality and consistency.

I'm naturally a peacemaker, and that can be Christlike. But sometimes keeping the peace is just conflict avoidance.

Yes, Jesus calmed the storm. But He also rocked the boat! Jesus didn't avoid conflict; He often caused it. Why? Because Jesus knew that conflict, not comfort, is the catalyst for growth.

Orson Welles gives a famous speech in *The Third Man*:

> In Italy, for thirty years under the Borgias, they had warfare, terror, murder, and bloodshed—but they produced Michelangelo, Leonardo da Vinci, and the Renaissance. In Switzerland, they had brotherly love, they had five hundred years of democracy and peace, and what did that produce? The cuckoo clock.[14]

My apologies to Swiss readers, but I rest my case!

One of the biggest mistakes I made as a young leader was trying to make everyone comfortable, but in the long run that doesn't do anybody any favors. I've since redefined my job description as a pastor. My job is to comfort the afflicted and afflict the comfortable, and the latter is not less loving than the former. It's more so!

Comforting the afflicted is love.

Afflicting the comfortable is tough love.

It is so much easier to just avoid conflict, isn't it? So we delay discipline, but in the long run that hurts more than it helps. Or we postpone tough conversations because we lack the emotional energy or courage.

Tough love demands tough decisions, tough conversations.

Jesus could have healed any day of the week, but He often chose the Sabbath. Why? Because He knew it'd be twice as fun! Why not kill two birds with one stone? Heal sick bodies while getting under the thin skin of the self-righteous Pharisees. Jesus knew it would get their goat, and that's why He did it. He was goading them. And that's what you do when you love someone. It's called *tough love*.

The words of the wise are like goads.[15]

A goad was a spiked stick used for driving cattle. Sometimes we have to say something *hurtful* in order to be *helpful*. If we fail to confront someone in their sin, we settle for the status quo. And that's not loving! If we really love them, if we really believe in them—then we goad them like a cattle driver. Now, let me nuance this a little bit, because it's *not* a license to hurt people.

You have to use the right words, at the right time, in the right spirit. If you have an agenda, keep your hurtful words to yourself. If you're simply venting your frustration or saying something that will make you feel better about yourself, then don't bother, because it will backfire.

You must genuinely have the other person's best interest at heart. And bookend your goading with lots of affirmation. That's how you speak the truth in love.[16]

As I look back on my life, you know who I respect the most? It's not those who "took it easy on me." It's those who pushed me to my potential, then pushed me past it. I didn't always like it at the time, but their goading led to growth.

Who do you need to goad?

And who have you licensed to goad you?

Playing the man doesn't allow pussyfooting. Postponing tough conversations only makes them more difficult. It also robs us of the opportunity for growth.

Iron doesn't sharpen iron without friction.

Toughskins

When I was a kid, I wore a brand of blue jeans called *Tough-skins*. The reinforced knees were a blend of Dacron Type 59 polyester and DuPont 420 nylon.[17] Those jeans came with a money-back guarantee that kids would outgrow them before they outwore them.

One of my frequently repeated prayers for my children is that they would have a *soft heart* toward God and toward their mom and dad. But that soft heart is best protected by *tough skin*. Thin skin doesn't cut it—it's too often injured, too easily offended.

One of my annual rituals is choosing a verse of the year. The verse I chose a few years ago was Proverbs 19:11: "It is to one's glory to overlook an offense." It was the same year I released a book, *The Circle Maker*, which has sold more copies than any of my other books but has also garnered its fair share of criticism.[18] It's no fun being falsely accused of false teaching or false motives. And I could have swallowed that pill and let it poison my spirit, but I made a decision to overlook the offense. My goal that year was to be *unoffendable*.

Don't let an arrow of criticism pierce your heart unless it first passes through the filter of Scripture.[19] No one is above rebuke, and we're all imperfect. So if the criticism is valid, repent. But if it's not, don't swallow the pill, because it will poison your spirit. Overlook the offense! You'll be more of a man because of it. Playing the man requires tough skin, and it's absolutely necessary if you want to play business, play politics, play sports, or even play marriage.

When I was in junior high school, I was called a few names that aren't fit for print. I'm sure you experienced this too. No one *graduates* from junior high—they survive! But as I look back on it, I think it prepared me for real life by teaching me how to prove the naysayers wrong. Now, please don't use that as an excuse for name-calling. Bullying is a legitimate issue. When I was a kid, physical bullying was a real problem. Add social media to the mix, and it has gotten even uglier. Either way, there is no place for it. Nothing is more cowardly than bullying.

That said, I wonder if our culture of political correctness has left us too thin-skinned. Again, I'm not advocating for careless, thoughtless, heartless insults. But when political correctness becomes the Golden Rule, speaking truth becomes bigotry. Truth is crucified in the name of tolerance, undermining civil debate, conscientious objection, and religious conviction.

We live in a culture where it's wrong to say something is wrong. And I think that's wrong! Remaining silent on a subject that God has spoken about isn't loving—it's cowardly. And when we fail to use our voice, we lose our voice. We as the church should be more known for what we're *for* than what we're *against*. But playing the man requires standing up for what you believe in, even if you're standing alone.

A few diagnostic questions: When was the last time you were criticized? If it's been awhile, it should make you nervous. Why? Because it probably means you're maintaining the status quo rather than challenging it. You can't make a difference without making waves, and some people in the boat won't like it. So be it. Rock the boat anyway. Also, how easily offended are you? If the answer is *easily*, then you need to man up. When you take offense, you become defensive. And the second you become defensive, the kingdom of God stops advancing through you. Playing the man means playing

34

offense with your life. In marriage, playing offense is called romance. With your kids, it's the difference between reactive and proactive parenting. In the workplace, it's bringing your A-game attitude Monday through Friday, nine to five.

Jesus was constantly badgered by the religious paparazzi; He was apprehended by a self-righteous mob that chanted, "Crucify him."[20] Then He was flogged, mocked, and nailed to a cross by Roman soldiers.

Question: What didn't Jesus do?

Answer: Defend Himself.

Jesus was still playing offense on the cross. He prayed, "Father, forgive them, for they do not know what they are doing."[21] If you are defensive, then figure out who you need to forgive. Start playing offense by praying for them!

Blood, Sweat, and Tears

Real men cry.

Ending a chapter titled "Tough as Nails" on that note feels a little funny, but I think it's an appropriate ending. If nothing is tougher for men than baring their souls and revealing their true feelings, then a true tough guy is someone who does just that.

In twenty years of leading National Community Church, I've tried to be strong and courageous. And that often means putting on a brave face and soldiering on. But if you surveyed our staff, I bet many of them would point to moments when I broke down and cried as the most meaningful, the most powerful.

I remember being emotionally wrecked once by a question during a session at the Catalyst Conference in Atlanta, Georgia. I took our staff to Catalyst for thirteen years straight, but this one moment ranks above the rest. Craig Groeschel asked the question: "Does your heart break for the things that break the heart of God?" My honest answer was no. My heart had become calloused, not just my skin. So we delayed our reservation at P. F. Chang's to have a come-to-Jesus meeting with our staff. We confessed. We cried. And not unlike the way a broken bone heals, my spirit became even stronger in the place where it had been broken.

I'm not saying you have to wear your emotions on your sleeve. But we're men, not automatons. And sometimes crying is leading.

"Jesus wept."[22]

It's every kid's favorite memory verse—two words! But those two words speak volumes about Jesus. The original language indicates intensity. This wasn't a single teardrop rolling down His cheek—this was a meltdown! Jesus lost it, and I love this dimension of who He is.

Jesus got sad. Jesus got mad. Then Jesus got even, raising Lazarus from the dead.

Good leadership takes blood, sweat, and tears. You have to make sacrifices—blood. You have to work hard—sweat. But you also have to lead with empathy—tears. And you can't fake this dimension of leadership!

When was the last time your wife saw you cry?

How about your kids?

What about your friends?

If it's been awhile, you're probably repressing something. And repression usually leads to obsession or depression. Your lack of vulnerability isn't courageous, it's cowardly!

Toughen up.

Tear up.

Play the man!

2

A Gentleman and a Scholar

The Second Virtue of Manhood:
Childlike Wonder

> When I became a man, I put the ways of child-
> hood behind me.
>
> —1 Corinthians 13:11

October 14, 1912
Milwaukee, Wisconsin

In October 1912, Teddy Roosevelt was campaigning for the White House when a would-be assassin shot him point-blank with a .32-caliber pistol. The bullet lodged two inches deep in his chest, but that didn't stop the Bull Moose from making his speech. "The bullet is in me now," Roosevelt informed the audience, "so that I cannot make a very long speech."[1] Roosevelt spoke for fifty-three minutes! By the time he was done, he was standing in a pool of his own blood.

Teddy was a tough guy, which is one reason he ranks as my favorite president. Consider Roosevelt's resume of manliness.

He rode a moose, took down an armed cowboy during a barroom brawl, crossed a frozen river to chase boat thieves, worked a ranch in the Dakotas, flew a Wright brothers airplane, scaled the Matterhorn in the Swiss Alps, went on month-long African safaris, navigated uncharted parts of the Amazon River, led the charge up Kettle Hill during the Battle of San Juan, set up a boxing ring in the White House so he could spar with anybody who dared get in the ring with him, and was known to go skinny-dipping in the Potomac River while president.[2]

And that's the tip of the iceberg. Roosevelt wasn't one to sit back and let life happen to him. He played offense with his life, a hurry-up offense. It was like a two-minute drill every minute of every hour of every day.

The English statesman John Morley likened Roosevelt to Niagara Falls. "Their common quality, which photographs and paintings fail to capture, is a perpetual flow of torrential energy."[3]

One of Roosevelt's biographers, Edmund Morris, called it an "inhuman energy." His description of Roosevelt's nightly ritual is classic. The president would brush his teeth, jump into bed, put his revolver beside his pillow, and read a minimum of one book per night. "Then, there being nothing further to do," says Morris, "Theodore Roosevelt will energetically fall asleep."[4]

Teddy was a man's man, the Rough Rider himself. But he never lost his childlike approach to life. And that childlike wonder is the second virtue of manhood. Playing the man demands a certain degree of playfulness, which was epitomized by America's twenty-sixth president. Roosevelt wasn't afraid of leaving heads of state waiting in the West Wing while he finished up a game of hide-and-seek with his children in the East Wing. But his holy curiosity and child-like wonder may be best evidenced by his unrivaled reading habit—a habit that averaged five hundred books per year. And that was while fulfilling his duties as president. Oh, and he also managed to write thirty-five books.

Feeling a little lazy? Me too!

At first glance, manliness and childlikeness seem to be at odds with each other, but they're not.

For the record, I want to *die young* at a ripe old age![5]

Teddy Roosevelt was a fighter, no doubt. But he was also a *thinker*. And that's part and parcel of playing the man— brains and brawn. Roosevelt was a gentleman and a scholar, modeling the second virtue of manhood. He knew more about more things than perhaps anyone of his era. But the more you know, the more you know how much you don't know! True knowledge results in profound humility, which fuels childlike wonder.

This virtue certainly isn't exclusive to men, but I find it more lacking in men than in women. At some point, most men lose their childlike sense of wonder. That's the day we stop living and start dying. And while that may sound some-what sentimental, it's actually a stewardship issue.

According to neurologists, our brains have a storage capac-ity of approximately 2.5 petabytes.[6] That's the equivalent of recording three hundred million hours of high-definition tele-vision! Simply put, we have the capacity to learn something new every second of every minute of every hour of every day for thousands of lifetimes! We won't run out of hard drive space anytime soon. And the three-pound supercomputer inside our craniums runs on less power than a twenty-watt lightbulb.[7] Amazing, isn't it?

The-Know-It-All

More than a decade ago now, A. J. Jacobs set out on a quest to become the smartest person in the world. He read the entire *Encyclopedia Britannica* from A to Z—32 volumes; 33,000 pages; 44 million words!

After college, Jacobs had done a self-described "intellectual swan dive." He became a writer for *Entertainment Weekly*, which he attributes as part of the reason for his intellectual decline. "I crammed my cranium with pop culture jetsam," writes Jacobs. "This meant anything profound got pushed out."[8] One day it dawned on him that he knew more about Homer Simpson than Homer the ancient Greek poet. That's when he decided to do something about it, and thus began his quest.

I'm not advocating an intellectual feeding frenzy. Afer all, we already suffer from information overload. There is more information in one Sunday edition of the *New York Times* than the average person living in the Middle Ages would have consumed in an entire lifetime. I'm not convinced we need to *know more*, as much as we need to *do more with what we know*. That said, keep learning!

"Live as if you'll die tomorrow," said Mahatma Gandhi. "Learn as if you'll live forever."[9]

That's a good rule of thumb.

According to the Pew Research Institute, half of adults read fewer than five books per year. And men read 13 percent fewer books than women.[10] I don't know if you're above average or below average, but five books a year doesn't cut it. Especially since most men average twenty hours of ESPN per week, myself included.

The most important law of ecology is this: $L \geq C$.

For an organism to survive, the rate of learning must be equal to or greater than the rate of change happening around them. With the rate of change escalating, we must learn faster, learn better, and learn more.

In the words of futurist John Naisbitt, "Learning how to learn is the most precious thing we have in life."[11] I might argue that learning how to unlearn is actually primary, and learning how to learn is secondary. But one way or the other, it has to be both/and.

The word *disciple* comes from the Greek word *mathétés*. The root word means "the mental effort needed to think something through." So by definition, a disciple is someone who never stops learning.

Faith is not mindless.

Faith is mindful.

Half-minded is no better than halfhearted.

One-fourth of the Great Commandment involves the mind. And loving God with all of your mind includes the right brain and the left brain. It also includes the medial ventral prefrontal cortex—the seat of humor! No joking!

The Ultimate Gentleman

In his 1951 novel, *The Catcher in the Rye*, author J. D. Salinger writes, "You're a real prince. You're a gentleman and a scholar, kid."[12] The phrase traces back to eighteenth-century

England where scholarship was as celebrated as chivalry. But it was Salinger who brought it back into common usage.

This phrase prompts very different word associations—from Special Agent 007 James Bond to the Most Interesting Man in the World, Jonathan Goldsmith![13]

I think Jesus.

We don't often talk about Him in these terms, but if you apply Merriam-Webster's definition—"a man who treats other people in a proper and polite way"—then Jesus is the quintessence of what it means to be a gentleman.[14] No one treats women with more respect or more dignity than Jesus. When the Pharisees picked up stones to throw at the woman caught in adultery, Jesus came to her defense.[15] His actions spoke louder than His words: you can stone her *over My dead body!* Jesus did the same for the woman who anointed His feet. While the Pharisees whispered about her past sins, Jesus declared her sins forgiven![16]

Jesus wasn't afraid of offending Pharisees, and He never failed to honor the women in His life—even while facing death. While Jesus was enduring the most painful death known to man, his dying concern was for His mother. Jesus said to John, "Here is your mother."[17] From that day forward, John took care of Mary like she was his own mother.

Gentleness might be the most undervalued fruit of the Spirit, especially among men.[18] But make no mistake about it, gentleness is manliness and manliness is gentleness. Think of manliness and gentleness as the iron fist in the velvet glove.

I won't say much on the subject of chivalry, and I don't want to overspiritualize the issue, but it deserves one paragraph. I hold the door for women, whether or not they want me to. I carry my wife's luggage, pull out her chair for her to sit, and help her put on her coat. Does she need me to do this? No. No, she doesn't. I do it for *me* as much as I do it for *her*. It's my way of reminding myself of the gift God has given me and the importance of cherishing her. I don't think you have to enroll in etiquette classes at the Emily Post Institute, but gentlemanly manners are one way of honoring your bride.

Someday someone will ask my daughter for her hand in marriage. And I've been praying for that lucky man for many years. But I hope he asks me for my blessing first. Call me old-fashioned, but that's the protocol I followed. My father-in-law was also my pastor, which made it twice as scary. When I finally mustered the courage to ask him, he said, "Let me pray about it." No kidding. Then he forgot to get back with me for a week! I now refer to that week as my *holy week*.

Genius

Jesus is a gentleman. He is also a genius.

"Today we think people are smart who make light bulbs and computer chips and rockets out of stuff already provided," says Dallas Willard. "He made the stuff."[19]

We overlook Jesus's genius because we assume His omniscience, but Jesus had to learn the Torah like every other Jewish boy. He also had to learn reading, writing, and arithmetic. Jesus obviously excelled, as evidenced by the fact that He impressed the religious leaders with His questions at twelve years of age. But Jesus had to climb the learning curve just like we do.

My academic background is somewhat scattered. I split my undergraduate education between the University of Chicago and Central Bible College. Then I pursued three graduate degrees in theology. I wouldn't trade one of my theology classes, but they would have been far less meaningful without my course of study at the U of C. In fact, my all-time favorite class was in immunology at the University of Chicago Hospital Center. I don't think my professor believed in God, but I walked out praising God for hemoglobin, immunoglobulin, and type T lymphocytes every single week. Each class was an exegesis of Psalm 139:14: "I am fearfully and wonderfully made."

I subscribe to Albert Einstein's school of thought: "Science without religion is lame, religion without science is blind."[20] If all truth is God's truth, then every "ology" is a branch of theology! If you want to know the Creator better, get to know His creation. Every facet of creation reveals something about His power, wisdom, and grace.

I'm not suggesting that you need to pursue a PhD in one of the sciences, but it might not hurt to cross-pollinate and learn a little something from different disciplines. And in that respect, Solomon sets the bar.

> God gave Solomon wisdom and very great insight. . . . He spoke three thousand proverbs and his songs numbered a thousand and five. He spoke about plant life, from the cedar of Lebanon to the hyssop that grows out of walls. He also spoke about animals and birds, reptiles and fish. From all nations people came to listen to Solomon's wisdom, sent by all the kings of the world, who had heard of his wisdom.[21]

King Solomon was a Renaissance man twenty-five hundred years before the Renaissance. His wisdom wasn't confined to theology; he had extensive knowledge ranging from botany to entomology to herpetology. Evidently he was interested in everything. And perhaps that's why kings and queens from all over the ancient world sought an audience with him.

"It is the glory of God to conceal a matter," said Solomon. "To search out a matter is the glory of kings."[22] Francis Bacon, a sixteenth-century English philosopher, had a fascinating take on this proverb:

> Solomon, although he excelled in the glory of treasure and magnificent buildings, of shipping and navigation, of fame and renown, yet he maketh no claim to any of those glories, but only to the glory of inquisition of truth; for so he saith, "The glory of God is to conceal a thing, but the glory of the king is to find it out"; as if, according to the innocent play of children, the Divine Majesty took delight to hide his works, in the end to have them found out; and as if kings could not obtain a greater honour than to be God's play-fellows in that game.[23]

We are God's playfellows.

That's part of what it means to play the man!

Have you ever hidden something from your children with the hope of them finding it? So they can experience the joy of discovery? That's what God does with us. To us, science seems like science. To God, it's a game of hide-and-seek. God has hidden clues about His character in macroscopic galaxies and microscopic atoms. It's our job—our joy—to discover them. And with each discovery, we gain a greater revelation and a greater appreciation of the Creator and His creation.

Empty Worship

During a rather fascinating TED talk, an expert in visual perception named Ed Seckel showed the audience a wide variety of images. One of them was a stenciled drawing of a couple intimately embracing. The audience immediately recognized what it was, but according to Seckel, children have no clue! Why? Because they have no prior memory to associate with it. Some of the kids said they saw nine dolphins![24]

You can't see what you don't know!

In his mind-bending book *Mozart's Brain and the Fighter Pilot*, Richard Restak shares a profound truism: learn more, see more.

> The richer my knowledge of flora and fauna of the woods, the more I'll be able to see. Our perceptions take on richness and depth as a result of all the things that we learn. What the eye sees is determined by what the brain has learned.[25]

When astronomers look into the night sky, they have a greater appreciation for the constellations, stars, and planets. They see more because they know more. When musicians listen to a symphony, they have a greater appreciation for the chords, melodies, and instrumentation. They hear more because they know more. When sommeliers sample a wine, they have a greater appreciation for the flavor, texture, and origin. They taste more because they know more.

Now, juxtapose that with this:

> You Samaritans worship what you do not know.[26]

The Samaritans were worshiping God out of ignorance. And when we worship out of ignorance, our worship is empty. We don't even know who or what or why we're worshiping!

Have you ever been guilty of apologizing to your wife without really knowing what you're sorry about? You just want to end the argument! I've been guilty of this a time or two, and sometimes my wife calls my bluff. Lora will ask me what I'm sorry about, and she's got me dead to rights. I have no clue what I'm sorry about. I'm just sorry!

That kind of apology is disingenuous, isn't it? If you don't even know what you're sorry about, it's an *empty apology*. And many of us worship God the same way. We sing the words we see on a screen, but do we really know what they mean? If God interrupted our singing and asked us why we're singing what we're singing, we'd be speechless.

Jesus offers a solution:

> God is Spirit, and his worshipers must worship in the spirit and in truth.[27]

We think of spiritual and intellectual pursuits as mutually exclusive endeavors, but they are one and the same. Great love is born of great knowledge. In fact, your knowledge is your worship ceiling!

Knowledge does not automatically translate into worship. But in some respects, quality of worship is determined by quantity of knowledge. The more you know, the more you have to worship.

Learn more, worship more.

Cum Laude

I don't think you have to graduate *summa cum laude* to play the man. But you shouldn't graduate *thank the laude* either! Part of manning up is studying to "show yourself approved." And it starts with the Word of God. Be a man of your word, but more important, be a man of the Word.

Paul exhorts his spiritual son Timothy: "Study to show yourself approved unto God, a workman that needs not to be ashamed."[28]

Paul combines the words *work* and *man* to create a wonderful compound—*workman*. A workman is someone who shows up every day, a blue-collar approach to the Bible that digs into the Word and then keeps digging.

Did you know that the kings of Israel were required to make a copy of the Law in their own handwriting? Then they were instructed to keep it on their person at all times. And, finally, they were told to read it all the days of their lives! Why? So they would revere the Lord and not think of themselves as being better than their fellow Israelites.[29]

Here's my advice: *act like a king.*

The Word of God is preventative medicine for whatever ails you. Take a daily dose. It'll make you smarter, for starters. But what's unique about the Bible is that you don't just read it; it reads you. It's a mirror that reveals who you are and who you can become in Christ. You can't play the man without being a man of the Word. If you don't have a reading plan, download one.[30] Then work the plan. But don't stop there.

Paul writes, "When you come, bring the cloak that I left with Carpus at Troas, and my scrolls, especially the parchments."[31]

It seems like a throwaway verse, but it speaks volumes about Paul. He was one of the most learned men of the first century and the author of much of the New Testament. Paul could have coasted to the intellectual finish line, but he was a lifelong learner! We don't know what his reading list consisted of, but he turned his jail cell into a reading room.

It might seem like a stretch, but I think it's reasonable to take a book with you wherever you go. And that includes the bathroom. The average man could read a book a month if he simply put a book in his bathroom. And I'm guessing that some of you have even more potential than that!

In the tenth century, the grand vizier of Persia, Abdul Kassem Ismael, took his 117,000-volume library with him wherever he went. It was organized and carried by a caravan of four hundred camels trained to walk in alphabetical order![32]

There are no excuses, guys. Especially when we can fit that many books on one digital device of our choosing.

The Youth Stone

Before my son Parker's thirteenth birthday, I spent several weeks planning a pretty elaborate Rite of Passage that I'll detail in the last chapter. It was the culmination of his year-long Discipleship Covenant, which included twelve books of my choosing.

I decided to stage the event at one of our favorite places in DC—Roosevelt Island. It's a ninety-acre island in the middle of the Potomac River, across from Georgetown. We did quite a bit of hiking and picnicking at Roosevelt Island when the kids were growing up, so it was symbolic of his youth. I also knew it was a place we could go back to over the years—a touchstone in his journey from boyhood to manhood.

After deciding on Roosevelt Island, I did some reconnaissance. I knew we could rent kayaks in Georgetown, but I had to figure out where to land. Then I staged each of his uncles at different points on the trail. Each uncle gave Parker a letter with lessons learned during their teen years, a symbolic gift, and a stump speech. Finally, I mapped out where we would all convene after his Rite of Passage walk—the statue of Teddy Roosevelt himself.

Behind the statue of Roosevelt stood two large granite stones. One was titled "Youth." The other was titled "Manhood." Could there be a more perfect place for a Rite of Passage?

On the day of the passage, I had Parker spend a few minutes meditating on each stone. And without him knowing it, I clicked a few pictures to capture the moment.

Each stone contains a compilation of quotes from Roosevelt's writings:

Youth

I WANT TO SEE YOU GAME BOYS, I WANT TO SEE YOU BRAVE AND MANLY AND I ALSO WANT TO SEE YOU GENTLE AND TENDER. BE PRACTICAL AS WELL AS GENEROUS IN YOUR IDEAS. KEEP YOUR EYES ON THE STARS BUT REMEMBER TO KEEP YOUR FEET ON THE GROUND. COURAGEOUS HARD WORK, SELF-MASTERY, AND INTELLIGENT EFFORT ARE ALL ESSENTIAL TO BE SUCCESSFUL IN LIFE. ALIKE FOR THE NATION AND THE INDIVIDUAL, THE ONE INDISPENSABLE REQUISITE IS CHARACTER.

A few years later I put together a similar Rite of Passage for Josiah. After meditating on the youth stone for a few minutes, I asked him which words meant the most to him. His favorite phrase was mine too: "Keep your eyes on the stars."

I love that phrase for a few reasons.

"Youth," Theodore Roosevelt Memorial,
Theodore Roosevelt Island

First, it reminds me of God telling Abraham to get out of his tent and look up at the stars.[33] Why? Because as long as Abraham was in the tent, he had an eight-foot ceiling! But the second he stepped outside, the sky was the limit.

Second, it reminds me of the camping trip my sons and I took to kick off Parker's Year of Discipleship. My most vivid memory is lying on our backs in a wide-open field on a cloudless night. We did some serious stargazing. Then

Josiah, who was only six years old at the time, said, "Look, Dad, a moving star!" He was so excited that I didn't have the heart to tell him we call those "airplanes."

The Manhood Stone

After meditating on the words from the youth stone for a few minutes, I had Parker and Josiah cross the threshold and spend a few minutes in front of the manhood stone. When they did, it was like their lives flashed before my eyes!

Manhood

A MAN'S USEFULNESS DEPENDS UPON HIS
LIVING UP TO HIS IDEALS INSOFAR AS HE CAN.
IT IS HARD TO FAIL BUT IT IS WORSE
NEVER TO HAVE TRIED TO SUCCEED.
ALL DARING AND COURAGE, ALL IRONED
ENDURANCE OF MISFORTUNE MAKE FOR A
FINER AND NOBLER TYPE OF MANHOOD.
ONLY THOSE ARE FIT TO LIVE WHO DO
NOT FEAR TO DIE, AND NONE ARE FIT
TO DIE WHO HAVE SHRUNK FROM THE
JOY OF LIFE AND THE DUTY OF LIFE.

I love the phrase "ironed endurance." And I can't help but wonder if Roosevelt was tipping his cap to King Solomon's proverb—"Iron sharpens iron."[34]

On April 10, 1899, Teddy Roosevelt stood before the Hamilton Club in Chicago and delivered a speech titled "The Strenuous Life." It was actually more of a sermon than a speech. In it Roosevelt stated,

I wish to preach, not the doctrine of ignoble ease, but the doctrine of the strenuous life, the life of toil and effort, of

"Manhood," Theodore Roosevelt Memorial,
Theodore Roosevelt Island

labor and strife; to preach the highest form of success which comes, not to the man who desires mere easy peace, but to the man who does not shrink from danger, from hardship, or from bitter toil, and who out of these wins the splendid ultimate triumph.[35]

Based on everything you've read about Roosevelt so far, you might be tempted to think he was born with hair on his chest. But by all accounts, Teddy was a mama's boy. Even into his teen years, he was a one-hundred-pound weakling who suffered from severe asthma. But Roosevelt made a defining decision that his physical disabilities would not deter or defer his dreams. He set out to remake his body through exercise. And he did the same exact thing with his mind.

Before entertaining guests, Roosevelt would read up on whatever subject matter they might be interested in. This enabled him to become quite the conversationalist. And I would suggest that it was one way in which Roosevelt loved his neighbor as himself—he showed genuine interest in their interests.

Childlikeness

Sir John Kirk, a nineteenth-century British naturalist, once said that if he had his way, there would always be a little child positioned in the heart of London—perhaps in the precincts of Westminster Abbey or St. Paul's Cathedral. And no one would be allowed to contest a seat in Parliament or become a candidate for public office until he had spent a day with that child and passed an examination in the child's novel methods of thought, feeling, and expression.[36]

That's *brilliant*!

Of course, God proposed this idea two thousand years ago. He positioned a child at the center of His kingdom. Or maybe I should say the entrance—you can't even get into the kingdom without becoming like a child. In the kingdom of God, childlikeness ranks right behind Christlikeness. And I would argue that they are synonyms.

Now, let me flip the coin.

Childlikeness = good.

54

Childishness = bad.

The apostle Paul writes,

> When I was a child, I talked like a child, I thought like a child, I reasoned like a child. When I became a man, I put the ways of childhood behind me.[37]

What does it mean to put childhood behind?

I certainly don't think it means losing our childlike sense of wonder or sense of humor. Again, playfulness is part of playing the man. I think Paul is talking about childish self-centeredness. When you're a baby, the whole world revolves around you. The world exists to meet your needs! But at some point, you need a Copernican revolution. If you try to make the world revolve around you, you'll be miserable! You've got to get over yourself so you can get on with whatever it is that God has called you to do!

Paul uses three verbs—*talk*, *think*, and *reason*. The challenge is this: the part of the brain responsible for consequential thinking, the frontal cortex, doesn't fully develop in men until their midtwenties.[38] So two-thirds of the battle is dealing with a maturing mind that is incapable of meeting the demands of manhood.

Simply put, teenage boys are at an intellectual disadvantage when it comes to consequential thinking. I was one of them, and so were you! We did dumb stuff, even by our own standards!

When I was in high school, I got pulled over by the police thirteen times. No kidding! Somehow I managed to get only two tickets. Not a bad batting average. I was a dumb driver, and the dumbest move I ever made was trying to drive through a twelve-foot snowdrift in a shopping mall parking lot. I backed up my 1985 Dodge Colt about thirty yards, shifted from economy to power mode, and put the pedal to the metal. When I hit the snowdrift at about 35 mph, my friends tell me it was like a snow bomb exploded.

For the record, you *cannot* drive through a snowdrift. I ended up on top of it, with my car tilted to one side, so I had to climb out of the passenger's side. The look on the face of the tow truck driver said it all: *How'd you get up there?* I'll tell you how: by not thinking consequentially. I also didn't think through the fact that all the snow packed into the front grill and undercarriage of my car would melt in the garage overnight, leaving a pool of water that would raise my parents' eyebrows!

If you want to play the man, here are two critical questions to ask yourself:

1. How can I become more childlike?
2. How can I become less childish?

If you only figure out one of those questions, you'll be half the man you could be.

Wonder

One of my goals as a father is to infuse my children with childlike wonder. That's why I included an intellectual component to the Discipleship Covenant. The goal isn't learning, it's the love of learning! I assigned a broad range of books, including fiction and nonfiction, because I wanted to instill a holy curiosity toward all of life all their lives!

One of my role models when it comes to wonder is Arthur Gordon. I read his wonderful book *Wonder* on our fifteenth anniversary trip to Italy, making it all the more meaningful. In fact, we saw one of the natural wonders of the world—the Blue Grotto off the coast of Capri. That book awakened me to wonder like few others, but one chapter in particular caught my fancy, "The Night the Stars Fell."

As a small boy, Arthur Gordon's family spent their summers at a seaside cottage. Late one night, after Arthur had fallen asleep, his father came into his room, picked him up out of bed, and carried him down to the beach. Then he told a half-asleep Arthur to look up into the night sky and watch. Just as his father said it, a shooting star streaked across the sky. Then another. And another. His father explained to him that on certain nights in August, the sky would put on a far greater fireworks display than any Fourth of July celebration.

Six decades later it would still rank as one of the most magical moments of Gordon's life! Reflecting on his father's influence, Gordon said that his dad believed that a new experience was more important for a small boy than an unbroken night of sleep.

"I had the usual quota of playthings," said Arthur, "but these are forgotten now. What I remember is the night the stars fell, the day we rode in a caboose, the time we tried to skin the alligator, the telegraph we made that really worked."[39]

What will your kids remember from their childhood?

It won't be the things you bought for them! And it probably won't be the things you preplanned as a parent. It will be the improvisational moments that can be identified only by a father's sixth sense. It's your job to create and capture those moments. And if you do, your kids will remember them sixty years hence!

Arthur Gordon captured his father's essence this way: "My Father had, to a marvelous degree, the gift of opening doors for his children, of leading them into areas of splendid newness. This, surely, is the most valuable legacy we can pass on to the next generation: not money, not houses or heirlooms, but a capacity for wonder and gratitude, a sense of aliveness and joy."[40]

Our lives are not just measured in minutes. They are measured in moments—those moments when wonder invades our ordinary reality.

Carpe wonder!

Small Enough

I recently toured the White House grounds during the annual Spring Garden Tour. As I walked by the Oval Office, it jogged my memory of one more Teddy Roosevelt story. One night he and his naturalist friend William Beebe went out on the White House lawn to look at the stars. Locating a faint spot of light in the lower left-hand corner of the Pegasus constellation, Roosevelt said, "That is the Spiral Galaxy of Andromeda. It is as large as our Milky Way. It is one of one hundred million galaxies. It is seven hundred and fifty thousand light-years away. It consists of a hundred billion suns, each larger than our own sun." Roosevelt and Beebe marveled at those facts for a moment. Then, almost like a little child, the president said, "Now I think we feel small enough, let's go to bed."[41]

A hundred years later, astrophysicists estimate the existence of at least eighty billion galaxies, which should make us feel even smaller!

"The chief proof of a man's real greatness," said Sherlock Holmes, "lies in the perception of his smallness."[42]

A big man knows how small he is, and that sense of smallness makes him appreciate how big God is. The true measure of a man isn't how much he knows; it's how much he does with what he knows.

A scholar knows how much he knows, and lets everybody know it. A gentleman and a scholar knows how much he doesn't know. He cares less about being *right* than about being *righteous*. He loves asking questions more than giving answers.

He's driven by a childlike wonder to know as much as he can about as much as he can. Why? So he can worship God as much as he can.

Play the man!

3

Unbroken

The Third Virtue of Manhood:
Will Power

I am responsible.
—1 Samuel 22:22

May 27, 1943
South Pacific Ocean

In 1943, an Army Air Force's B-24 bomber, the *Green Hornet,*
was on a search and rescue mission when its engine malfunc-
tioned and crashed into the Pacific Ocean. Second Lieuten-
ant Louie Zamperini survived the crash, but he was lost at
sea. Finding a life raft in an ocean that covers one-third of
planet Earth is far more difficult than finding a needle in a
haystack. For forty-seven days Louie survived on rainwater,
raw fish, and will power.

The equatorial current carried his raft two thousand miles into Japanese-controlled waters, where he became a prisoner of war. When Mutsuhiro "the Bird" Watanabe, one of WWII's most wanted war criminals, discovered that Louie was a former US Olympian, he took special pleasure in torturing his mind, body, and spirit. If you can stomach it, read the book or watch the film *Unbroken*.

Shortly after his plane crashed, Louie was classified KIA—killed in action—by the US military. After all, how could anyone survive a crash like that or survive at sea that long? Louie was skin and bones when he was captured, having wasted away to less than half his original body weight—a "dead body breathing."[1] The legs that had nearly broken a four-minute mile could barely hold him upright. And after two years in the Japanese war camps, Louie was even worse off.

Louie survived daily beatings with a bamboo kendo stick. He survived 220 punches in the face. He survived the mocking guards who made him dance the Charleston while almost completely naked. He survived bitter cold and brutal heat. He survived forced labor, shoveling twenty tons of coal per day at the Tokyo rail yard. He survived cesspit duty, carrying buckets of nauseating waste.

Through it all, Louie played the man. He survived hell on earth and lived another seventy years after his rescue and release.

How did he do it?

He endured two years in a Japanese war camp the same way he survived forty-seven days at sea and the same way he trained for the five-thousand-meter race in the 1936 Berlin Olympics. Louie Zamperini is a rare breed of man, a man who models the third virtue of manhood—*will power*.

You can't play the man without it!

It's will power that kept Zamperini alive.

It's will power that kept Polycarp from recanting.

It's will power that kept Christ on the cross.

Response-Ability

In a Nazi death camp, an Austrian psychiatrist named Viktor Frankl was stripped of his possessions, his clothes, even his name. He was reduced to a number—prisoner 119,104. His mother, brother, and wife would not survive the death camp.

After his liberation, Frankl wrote a book for the ages—*Man's Search for Meaning*. In the book, Frankl reveals the secret to his survival: "Everything can be taken from a man but one thing: the last of human freedoms—to choose one's attitude in any given set of circumstances."[2]

Were Louie Zamperini or Viktor Frankl responsible for the suffering they endured? Absolutely not. They were victims of evil incarnate. But while they may not have been responsible, they were *response-able*. And that little hyphen makes all the difference in the world. There is no situation under the sun in which your ability to respond can be taken away from you. You may not control your circumstances, but you control your reactions to them. And that is what sets the men apart from the boys!

Taking response-ability doesn't mean admitting fault. It means *making the most of any and every situation you find yourself in*. And that requires tremendous will power in difficult circumstances.

What do you do when your marriage is falling apart at the seams? When your work environment goes from bad to worse? When an addiction spins out of control?

First of all, take heart.

In this world you will have trouble. But take heart! I have overcome the world.[3]

Second, take response-ability!
George Bernard Shaw, the great Irish playwright and political activist, said, "People are always blaming their circumstances for what they are. I don't believe in circumstances. The people who get on in this world are the people who get up and look for circumstances they want and if they can't find them, make them."[4]

Fear is letting your circumstances come between you and God.

Faith is letting God get between you and your circumstances.

Delayed Gratification

In 1972, a psychologist named Walter Mischel conducted a series of studies on delayed gratification, known as the Stanford Marshmallow Experiment. The original study was done at Bing Nursery School with children ages four to six. A single marshmallow was offered to each child, and if the child could resist eating it right away, he or she was promised two marshmallows instead of one.

A hidden camera allowed the researchers to observe the way in which children responded to that situation. Some kids grabbed the marshmallow the moment the researcher walked out of the room, while others mustered as much will power as they possibly could, employing a wide range of temptation-resisting tactics. The children sang songs, played games, covered their eyes, and even tried going to sleep.

The objective of the experiment was to see if the children's ability to delay gratification correlated to long-term academic achievement, so the academic records of the 216 children who participated were tracked all the way through high school. When the longitudinal results were cross-referenced with delayed gratification times, researchers found that the kids who exhibited the ability to delay gratification longer were more academically accomplished. They scored, on average, 210 points higher on the SAT. The marshmallow test was twice as powerful an indicator of academic achievement as IQ.[5] The delayed gratification kids were also more self-reliant and socially competent. They took initiative more frequently and handled stress more effectively. And in a follow-up study done four decades after the initial research, they had higher incomes, stronger marriages, and happier careers.[6]

If you want to be successful at anything, at everything—*delay gratification*. Of course, it's easier said than done! But the key is will power.

The Secret Sauce

When I was in my twenties, I spent a week with Jack Hayford at his School of Pastoral Nurture. That week transformed the trajectory of my ministry. Jack is now in his eighties, and his wit and wisdom are off the charts! At a pastors gathering not long ago, Jack shared his secret sauce. It's so simple yet so profound: *make decisions against yourself.*

We want success without sacrifice, but life doesn't work that way. Success will not be shortchanged. You have to pay the price, and it never goes on sale. The best decision you can make *for* yourself is making decisions *against* yourself. You have to discipline yourself to do the right things day in and day out, week in and week out, year in and year out. And if you do, the payoff is far greater than the price you paid. Nothing compounds interest like delayed gratification.

For two hours Jack detailed some of those defining and difficult decisions he had made. Some of them were focused on resisting temptation. They were right-or-wrong, black-or-white decisions. Others were matters of personal conviction. They wouldn't be wrong for anyone else, but they were for Jack. For example, Jack gave up chocolate, which certainly qualifies as a decision against yourself.

Jack would be the first person to say there is nothing wrong with chocolate. Thank God for chocolate—hot chocolate, chocolate fondue, and molten chocolate lava cake! But for nearly thirty years, Jack has not eaten chocolate. Why? Not because it's wrong, but because it's a personal decision, a personal conviction. He felt like God wanted him to steer clear of chocolate. So Jack made a decision against himself, and as you can imagine, it's helped him exercise self-control in other areas of his life.

If you want God's best, you can't just say no to what's wrong. You have to say no to second best. Good isn't good enough! That's what the apostle Paul is getting at when he writes,

> "Everything is permissible for me," but not everything is beneficial.[7]

This little distinction between *permissible* and *beneficial* is the difference between good and great. Don't settle for what's permissible. That's the path of least resistance. Go after greatness by going the extra mile!

Will power means not my will, but "your will be done."[8] It's a will that has been fully surrendered to the lordship of Jesus Christ. It's a sanctified stubborn streak that refuses to compromise its convictions.

Now, let's bring this idea down to earth.

If you want to get out of debt, you've got to make decisions against yourself financially. It's called sticking to a budget. If you want to get into shape, you've got to make decisions against yourself physically. Join the gym. If you want to grow spiritually, you've got to make decisions against yourself. Try fasting.

What decision against yourself do you need to make? If you have the courage to make it, it'll be the best thing you've ever done for yourself. If you don't believe me, ask a world-class athlete or renowned musician. The only way you become great at anything is by making decisions against yourself.

The "No" Muscle

The human body has more than six hundred skeletal muscles. And in case you care, they have the combined potential of lifting twenty-five tons if they were all leveraged at the same time, the same way! The hardest-working muscle is the heart, pumping twenty-five hundred gallons of blood through sixty thousand miles of veins, arteries, and capillaries every single day. The largest muscle is the gluteus maximus. And the strongest muscle is the masseter muscle in your jaw, which can exert two hundred pounds of force on your molars.

Those muscles exert power, giving you the strength to do what needs to be done. But only one muscle gives you the strength not to do what shouldn't be done. I call it the "no" muscle. And it's exercised only via will power.

It's the muscle you flex when you say no to sleep, no to sex, or no to dessert. It's not as easy to exercise as your pectorals, but the best way to bench press it is through a spiritual discipline called fasting. Fasting helps you not only break bad habits but also build will power. If you can say no to food, then you can say no to just about anything!

Jesus set the bar, fasting for forty days. And it's no coincidence that the first temptation He faced was a challenge from the devil to turn a stone into bread. But Jesus leveraged every ounce of will power in His possession, saying, "Man shall not live on bread alone."[9]

At its core, fasting is the way we declare our dependence on God—we need Him more than we need food itself. It takes tremendous will power to give up food, but it cultivates tremendous will power in other areas of our lives.

If you can exercise discipline physically, it'll help you practice the daily spiritual discipline of reading Scripture and vice versa. If you practice the spiritual discipline of prayer, it'll help you stick with your exercise regimen or diet plan.

Discipline begets discipline.

Twelve Legions

We find two Greek words used for "power" in Scripture, and they form an interesting yin and yang relationship. *Dunamis* is the power to do things beyond your natural ability. It's where we get our word *dynamite*. *Exousia* is the power not to do something that is within your power to do.

It takes *dunamis* to bench press two hundred pounds.

It takes *exousia* to stop at one Oreo.

Both types of power are important, but exousia is rarer. It's good old-fashioned will power, and it's the difference between playing the man and playing the fool.

Jesus walked on water and walked through walls. He healed the sick and raised the dead. His *dunamis* was off the charts. But His greatest victory was won with *exousia*. As Jesus hung on the cross, He said, "Do you think I cannot call on my Father, and he will at once put at my disposal more than twelve legions of angels?"[10]

A legion was the largest unit in the Roman military, consisting of six thousand soldiers. So Jesus had seventy-two thousand angels at His beck and call. Listen, *one* angel could have done the trick. Jesus could have exercised His *dunamis*, killing the soldiers who were killing Him. But instead of exercising His power, He exercised His will power.

The Lion of the Tribe of Judah let the Romans flog Him, mock Him, and spit on Him. The Ancient of Days let them rip off His robe and put a crown of thorns on His head. The Omnipotent One let them nail Him to a cross.

What kept Him there? Not seven-inch nails, that's for sure! It was *exousia* that kept Him on the cross. The same kind of *exousia* it takes to carry our crosses.

Temptation Island

First things first—no one is beyond temptation. No matter how mature you become spiritually, the undertow of temptation is trying to suck you under and drown you in lust or pride or guilt. Even Jesus wasn't beyond temptation.

> We do not have a high priest who is unable to empathize with our weaknesses, but we have one who has been tempted in every way, just as we are—yet he did not sin.[11]

Part of becoming like Christ is being tempted in every way, just like Jesus. And each time you pass a test, you graduate to the next level of spiritual maturity. So quit viewing temptation as a necessary evil. It's a golden opportunity for you to grow in character and prove yourself to Christ. Will you ace every test? No, you won't. But that's when you repent and repeat.

Overcoming temptation starts with recognizing your triggers.

For most guys, we get into trouble when we're tired, lonely, or bored. And King David is a great example of that. Why did he fall into sin with Bathsheba? I think he exposed himself to temptation the day he sent his army off to war but stayed home himself. Ironically, being on the sidelines was far more dangerous spiritually than being on the front line. David had too much time on his hands, and idle hands are the devil's workshop.

> In the spring, at the time when kings go off to war, David sent Joab out with the king's men and the whole Israelite army. They destroyed the Ammonites and besieged Rabbah. But David remained in Jerusalem.
>
> One evening David got up from his bed and walked around on the roof of the palace. From the roof he saw a woman bathing. The woman was very beautiful, and David sent someone to find out about her. The man said, "She is Bathsheba, the daughter of Eliam and the wife of Uriah the Hittite."[12]

This isn't rocket science.

David was lonely—he was home alone. David was bored—he was playing *Call of Duty* instead of doing his duty as commander in chief. And David was tired—the bewitching hour was evening time, after a long day of doing nothing.

Why was David walking around on his roof? Because he had nothing else to do! So instead of playing the man, he played the Peeping Tom.

The secret to not sinning is *not* not sinning.

The secret to sinning less is dreaming more! You need a God-sized dream that is bigger and better than whatever sinful temptation you face. You need a vision for your marriage that is better than internet pornography. You need a vision for your life that is bigger and better than selfish ambition.

That's how you get off Temptation Island.

Triggers

Jesus, full of the Holy Spirit, left the Jordan and was led by the Spirit into the wilderness, where for forty days he was tempted by the devil. He ate nothing during those days, and at the end of them he was hungry.[13]

Luke is Captain Obvious. Jesus was hungry after forty days of not eating? Really? The truth is, He was starving, which makes the first temptation very predictable. The devil tempted Him to turn a stone into bread—instant gratification. But Jesus didn't bite.

The enemy knows *how* to hit us where it hurts, and he also knows *when*. Is it any coincidence that the first temptation involved food? No. Jesus was most vulnerable in this regard. The enemy even tried to use Scripture to rationalize a compromise, but Jesus counterpunched with a left jab:

Man shall not live on bread alone.[14]

Ask yourself: Do you have a need that's not getting met? That's the target the enemy aims at. This is precisely why married couples must cultivate a healthy sex life. The best defense is a good offense. Perhaps that's why God gave newly married men a year off from work or responsibilities in Old Testament times—to cultivate that strong offense.

If a man has recently married, he must not be sent to war or have any other duty laid on him. For one year he is to be free to stay at home and bring happiness to the wife he has married.[15]

No exegesis necessary! What I love about this is that it's a *commandment*. More commandments, please!

I have a pastor friend who was teaching on the subject of sex right around the time Wilt Chamberlain claimed to have had twenty thousand sex partners. During his sermon, my friend announced, "I've had sex twenty thousand times, but it's been with the same woman." At the time he had been married sixteen years. Do the math! That works out to 3.425 times per day, seven days a week. Yeah, I don't think so!

Permission to speak frankly?

I haven't met too many men who feel like they're having too much sex. Rarely do I hear a guy say, "I just can't keep up with my wife." Those men may exist, but I bet they have a below-average libido. Not that there's anything wrong with that. However, many married men feel shortchanged in regard to sex, and that's a dangerous way to feel in any marriage. These men feel cheated, so they often use it as an excuse to cheat on their wives.

Nine times out of ten, we sin because we're trying to meet a *legitimate need* in an *illegitimate way*. We rationalize sin instead of taking response-ability for our situation.

There is no excuse for being unfaithful to your spouse—ever! That's the antithesis of playing the man!

Now, let's get down to brass tacks.

It starts with taking inventory of temptation. What are your triggers? Ask yourself *when*, *where*, and *how* it happens.

When do you give in to lustful thoughts? Is it late at night? Is it when you're traveling alone?

When do you lose your temper? Do you let your frustration from work boil over at home? Or are your angry outbursts the result of sexual frustration?

Once you identify your triggers, take a proactive step. For example, when at a hotel while traveling alone, ask the front desk person to remove the movie channels. Pull the plug so you can't pull the trigger. Cancel the subscription, cancel the magazine, or cancel the appointment.

You know what you need to do. Now do it.

Jesus was using hyperbole when He said to gouge out and throw away the eye that causes you to lust and to cut off the hand that causes you to sin.[16] Hyperbole shouldn't be taken literally, but it better be taken seriously. You have to take preventative measures.

It's unwise to flirt with temptation. You shouldn't even touch it with a ten-foot pole. Why? Because all the enemy needs is a foothold—one lie, one compromise, one click. And if you give him an inch, he'll take a mile.

Now, some good news.

First of all, you're not alone.

Second, you can do this.

No temptation has overtaken you except what is common to mankind. And God is faithful; he will not let you be tempted beyond what you can bear. But when you are tempted, he will also provide a way out so that you can endure it.[17]

I can't promise that you will bat a thousand. But you can win more battles with temptation than you lose. And there is always a way out. Of course, it might take you as long to get out as it did to get in. Can God deliver you in a day? No doubt about it. But you must behave accordingly and back up that deliverance day in and day out. How? Focus on healthy, positive daily disciplines so you don't fall back into the trap of temptation.

The Crags of the Wild Goats

When David was in his twenties, he was a political fugitive. Saul was hunting him down, trying to kill him, so David hid out in a place called the "Crags of the Wild Goats." That is precisely where I would have hid too, just so I could say it. It makes you feel like more of a man! "Where have you been?" someone might ask. "The Crags of the Wild Goats!" I would say. That's cooler than a man cave!

[Saul] came to the sheep pens along the way; a cave was there, and Saul went in to relieve himself. David and his men were far back in the cave. The men said, "This is the day the LORD spoke of when he said to you, 'I will give your enemy into

your hands for you to deal with as you wish.'" Then David
crept up unnoticed and cut off a corner of Saul's robe.[18]

This is classic, right? We don't know if Saul went number
one or number two, but either way, David was in the stall
next to him. Based on the fact that David had enough time
to cut off a corner of his robe, I'm guessing it was number
two! And this little fact is not insignificant.

If we're talking number two, David's integrity is far more
impressive. Why? Because this isn't a short-fused temptation.
David had time to think about it and act on it. In fact, his
men had enough time to lobby him to do it. It seemed like
a golden opportunity to kill the king and grab the crown,
but an opportunity *is not* an opportunity if you have to
compromise your integrity.

If you have to lie on a résumé or withhold information
during an interview process, it's not worth getting the job. If
you get the job by compromising your integrity, you'll likely
have to compromise your integrity to keep it.

Every man has defining moments in his life when his integrity is tested. We're tempted to take a shortcut, to turn
a stone into bread instead of baking a loaf. But it always
short-circuits God's good, pleasing, and perfect will.

Don't go there.

Forfeit "the opportunity" for the sake of your integrity.

David was a few inches and a few moments away from
becoming king of Israel. All he had to do was stab Saul in
the back, but David knew that Saul was anointed and appointed by God. It was against the law to kill the king, no
matter how bad the king was. God set Saul up, and God
could take him out. So David exercised tremendous *exousia*

by not taking matters into his own hands. Had he killed Saul, his fingerprints would have been all over it. And when we get our fingerprints all over something, it usually means we have taken matters into our own hands instead of putting them into the hands of almighty God.

Epic Integrity

We live in a culture that celebrates talent more than integrity, but we've got it backward. Talent depreciates over time, just like our bodies. Our physical strength and appearance diminish. We may even lose our minds. But we never have to lose our integrity. Integrity appreciates over time—over eternity!

Bobby Jones is one the greatest golfers in history and was the first player to win four majors in one year. But Jones was an even better person. He won thirteen majors before retiring at the age of twenty-eight, but it's the one he lost that set him apart. Jones took a one-shot penalty at the 1925 US Open, even though no one else saw him touch his ball with his club. Jones wasn't altogether certain he had touched the ball, and rules officials encouraged him not to take the penalty, but Jones assessed the penalty *just in case*. Jones lost the tournament by one stroke, but he kept his integrity intact. Winning the US Open wasn't worth a one-stroke penalty on his integrity.

That's epic integrity.

When tournament officials complimented him for his choice, Jones said, "You might as well praise me for not breaking into banks. There is only one way to play this game."[19] And there is only one way to play the man! Bobby Jones played by the rules. In so doing, he honored the integrity of the game.

And David was conscience-stricken for having cut off a corner of Saul's robe?[20]

Seriously? Saul was throwing spears at David, and David was beating himself up for cutting off a corner of Saul's robe. It's hard to believe, isn't it? But David was a man whose conscience was sensitized to the Holy Spirit.

The lesson? Don't cut corners.

You aren't defined by who you are when everyone is looking. You are defined by what no one sees, save the All-Seeing Eye. That's who you really are.

Your integrity is your legacy.

Your integrity is your destiny.

It's true of King David.

It's true of Bobby Jones.

It's true of you.

Play the man!

4

The Three-Headed Dragon

The Fourth Virtue of Manhood:
Raw Passion

From the days of John the Baptist until now the
kingdom of heaven suffers violence, and violent
men take it by force.

—Matthew 11:12 NASB

December 1874
Sierra Nevada Mountains

John Muir, naturalist extraordinaire, once charged a bear
just so he could study its running gait.[1] Is there anything else
you need to know about the man? That's about as crazy as
chasing a lion into a pit on a snowy day! Muir once took a
thousand-mile walk from Louisville, Kentucky, to New Orleans, Louisiana. Why? Just because. He explored sixty-five

glaciers in the Alaska territory—and sledded down some of them. And a century before Bear Grylls went adventuring with celebrities on his reality TV show *Running Wild*, John Muir took President Teddy Roosevelt camping in the shadow of El Capitan. And, of course, John Muir did all of this before REI, GPS, or 30,0000-BTU camping stoves!

If you've ever visited Yosemite National Park, you owe John Muir a thank-you. And if you haven't visited, you need to. Hiking to the top of Half Dome was life goal #89 for me, and it ranks as one of my all-time favorite hikes![2] And very appropriately, I hiked the *John Muir Trail* to get there.

John Muir embodied the virtues of manhood in a unique way. The patron saint of the American wilderness was a man on a mission. His vision, his passion, "was saving the American soul from total surrender to materialism."[3] Like John the Baptist before him, Muir saw himself as a prophet crying out in the wilderness, crying out *for* the wilderness. His goal? To immerse everyone he could in what he called "mountain baptism."

Starting at an early age, Muir read Scripture every single day. Actually, he did more than read it; he memorized the entire New Testament.[4] Then he turned his attention to the book of nature, or as he called it, "the invention of God."[5] Muir believed that the Creator was constantly revealing Himself through His creation, so he studied it with more childlike wonder than perhaps anyone before—or anyone since!

In 1874, Muir wrote an article for *Scribner's Magazine* titled "Wind-Storm in the Forests of the Yuba." Muir was staying at a friend's cabin nestled in the Sierra Nevada when a winter storm swept through the valley. Instead of seeking shelter, Muir sought adventure. Gale-force winds bent trees past their breaking point, snapping hundreds of trees in a matter of hours.

So what did John Muir do?

He located the tallest cluster of Douglas fir trees he could find, and then he climbed one of them to the very top. The hundred-foot tree swayed up to thirty degrees, from side to side, while Muir held on for dear life, feasting his senses on the sights, sounds, and smells of the earth, the wind, and the storm.

"On such occasions, nature always has something rare to show us," said Muir. "And the danger to life and limb is hardly greater than one would experience crouching deprecatingly beneath a roof."[6]

Most people live as if the purpose of life is to arrive safely at death, but not Muir. He had a passion for life that took no prisoners. And that's the fourth virtue of manhood—*raw passion*. It's a lust for life that doesn't settle for status or status quo. It's an insatiable energy that motivates you to live each day like it's the first day and the last day of your life. It's an infectious enthusiasm that can come only from being filled with the Holy Spirit to overflowing.

The word *enthusiasm* comes from the Greek roots *en* and *Theos*, meaning *in God*. So the more you get into God, and the more of God's Spirit that gets into you, the more impassioned you become.

The Third Baptism

I believe in baptism by immersion, but not just with water. I also believe in baptism by fire. It's the baptism John the Baptist prophetically pointed to—a baptism in the Spirit, by the Spirit.[7] Without it, we're below average. With it, it's game on. There is also a third baptism—a baptism into manhood.

Just as water baptism symbolizes our death to self and new life in Christ, the third baptism is a Rite of Passage from boyhood to manhood. It's a proving ground where mental toughness and physical toughness are tested to their limits. Without the test, a man never really knows for sure if he's man enough.

This is what is lacking in our culture, in our generation.

When I created the Discipleship Covenant and Year of Discipleship for my sons, I didn't think of it as a third baptism. Honestly, I was flying blind. But in retrospect, I see how it gave my boys a benchmark to shoot for. The three challenges—physical, intellectual, and spiritual—gave them a proving ground. They didn't need to prove anything to me. I love them no matter what. They needed to prove to themselves that they had what it takes to be a man.

I designed something similar for my daughter, Summer. When she was thirteen years old, we trained for the Escape from Alcatraz—a one-and-a-half-mile swim from Alcatraz Island to San Francisco through shark-infested waters. I actually got some backlash from people who called me a terrible parent. *How could I possibly put my daughter in that kind of danger?* First of all, there has never been a shark attack in the history of the event. Second, Summer is a stronger swimmer than I am. So if anyone would have been in danger, it probably would have been me! Plus, I would have been a much bigger target for any sharks that might have been lurking.

Unfortunately, the race got canceled just moments before we jumped off the boat and into the San Francisco Bay. Too much fog. Go figure! After the initial disappointment wore off, I realized Summer's willingness to even attempt that kind of feat at thirteen years old proved to be something she can build off of for the rest of her life!

A Standing Rebuke

Back to John Muir.

Citing the story of Muir climbing the Douglas fir tree, Eugene Peterson said Muir was "a standing rebuke against becoming a mere spectator to life, preferring creature comfort to Creator confrontation."[8] Peterson actually dubbed John Muir an "icon of Christian spirituality." That may seem like a stretch, but I think he's on to something.

Jesus had a wild side, and so should we—a sanctified wild side. And the best place to get in touch with your wild side is in the wilderness. We read the Bible through a sanitized, civilized lens. We focus almost exclusively on *what* Jesus said and did, not *when*, *where*, or *how*. If you focus on theology while ignoring geography, meteorology, or even neurology, you miss some amazing subplots.

Where did the transfiguration happen?

Scripture is explicit—a *high mountain*. And how did Jesus and His inner circle get there? By climbing it! We're not entirely sure which mountain Jesus summited, but Mount Hermon is one possibility—elevation 9,232 feet. That's not a fourteener, but it's not a walk in the park either!

"Foxes have dens and birds have nests," said Jesus, "but the Son of Man has no place to lay his head."[9] Translation: the disciples never got too comfortable for too long! They were always on the move and, sometimes, on the run! It was a "buckle your seat belt and keep your hands inside the ride at all times" roller coaster.

When was the last time you got outside your comfort zone physically, spiritually, or relationally? You tell me the last time you were uncomfortable, and I'll tell you the last time you grew! Growth only happens when we put ourselves into uncomfortable situations!

If you don't break down a muscle, it can't rebuild itself even stronger. And that's as true of emotional muscles as it is of physical muscles.

Emotional vulnerability is incredibly uncomfortable for most men, but that's how you develop intimacy in a relationship. Next time you're at dinner with your friends or with your wife, share something that makes you feel uncomfortable and see where the conversation goes. I bet it ends in a man hug with your friends or something even better with your wife.

Rawhide

If we did a word association test and I said "passion," what is the first thing that pops into your mind? For me it's Jesus walking into the temple with a homemade whip and throwing down Chuck Norris style! Jesus confronted the money changers, turned over tables, and led a stampede of animals out the exit.

I'm hearing the 1958 classic song "Rawhide" in my head.

When the melee was over, the disciples remembered an Old Testament prophecy that was fulfilled that day: "Zeal for your house will consume me."[10]

What Jesus did is amazing—He single-handedly turned the temple upside down. But just as amazing as what Jesus *did* is what the temple guard *did not do*! Temple guards were well-trained soldiers whose job was to keep people from doing what Jesus did. So why did the guard do nothing when Jesus started tearing up the place? The only explanation I can come up with is that they were either intimidated by His power or they submitted to His authority. Either way, Jesus performed an act of unparalleled passion. But for Jesus, it was par for the course.

Jesus may have been meek and mild, but He also had a wild side. He touched lepers, celebrated Samaritans, stopped storms, exorcised demons, ate with sinners, healed on the Sabbath, and turned funeral processions into parades! Then He died the way He lived—with pure passion. It's no coincidence that the final week of His life is synonymous with passion—Passion Week.

In the words of Dorothy Sayers,

> The people who hanged Christ never, to do them justice, accused him of being a bore—on the contrary, they thought him too dynamic to be safe. It has been left for later generations to muffle up that shattering personality and surround him with an atmosphere of tedium. We have very efficiently pared the claw of the Lion of Judah, certified him "meek and mild," and recommended him as a fitting household pet for pale curates and pious old ladies.[11]

When you follow in the footsteps of Jesus, His passion will refine you and define you. God doesn't just crucify our passions; He resurrects them and uses them for His purposes! As C. S. Lewis aptly observed, "Our Lord finds our desires not too strong, but too weak. We are half-hearted creatures, fooling about with drink and sex and ambition when infinite joy is offered us."[12]

Playing the man means playing hard—giving God everything you've got. It's leaving it all out on the court. The gold
standard is Colossians 3:23, which says,

> Whatever you do, work at it with all of your heart, as work-
> ing for the Lord.

A literal translation could read: "Do it like your life depends on it." In other words, give it *everything* you've got.
Don't just make a living. Make a life. Don't just earn a pay-
check. Go after the passions God has put in your heart. Half-
way is no way to live; you've got to go all in.

So what's standing in your way? The problem is as old as
Eden itself. Let's go all the way back to the opening act of
Scripture to review.

Act One, Scene One

Twenty-five years ago I had a sixty-second conversation I've
never forgotten. While speaking at a Teen Challenge Center
in Chicago, I met a man who had made some bad choices—he
struggled with drug and alcohol addiction and had a criminal
record to go with it. What I remember from that conversation is the acute psychological pain caused by something his
dad would say to him whenever he made a mistake: "What
the hell, ya stupid?" This man heard those words repeatedly
until they became the subconscious script of his life. I'm not
making excuses for the mistakes he made, but he was acting
out the lines his father had fed him his entire life.

For the record, if I ever met his dad, I think I'd give that
same line back to him.

This man needed a new script, and he got one from his heavenly Father. Of course, it takes time to read a new script, learn the lines, and get into character. This I know for sure: the Author and Perfecter of your faith wants to write His story through your life, but you have to give Him complete editorial control.

Scripture is so many things—it's our sword, our mirror, our map, and our manual. But I like to think of Scripture as a script. In fact, Scripture is our script cure. It's the way we flip the script of our lives!

You can't play the man if you don't know the script. It's how we get into character, the character of Christ. So let's rewind to the opening scene of the opening act of Scripture. And let's reverse engineer what went wrong.

In the realm of computer science, reverse engineering is analyzing a software source code in order to fix bugs, improve functionality, and repurpose a product. Reverse engineering Adam's original sin is no easy task, but it's the way we pop the hood on manhood.

First of all, call me Adam.

You and I are like Adam in every way, except for the fact that Adam probably didn't have a belly button. But in every other way, we are the spitting image of Adam, which is the image of God. The image of God is who we are at the core— the truest thing about us. It's what gives us the inkling to imagine, the capacity to cry, and the ability to laugh. And like Adam, we also have a sin nature. If the image of God is our original software, sin is the virus. Sin corrupts the entire archive, distorting the algorithm of what it means to be a man.

The good news is we still have the original source code that reveals God's original intent. The story of Adam is the key to reverse engineering our problems and our potential as men. Every man needs to fight three different tendencies—a Three-Headed Dragon. That might seem like a strange metaphor, but it's a biblical one. Our ancient foe is described as a dragon in the book of Revelation, and he does now what he did then.

> The dragon stood in front of the woman who was about to give birth, so that it might devour her child the moment he was born.[13]

It seems like a cryptic prophecy, but perhaps the obvious eludes us. You've had a target on your back since the day you were born. That doesn't need to scare you, because He that is in us is greater than he that is in the world.[14] But we ignore the enemy's tactics at our own peril. So let me name the heads of the Three-Headed Dragon, and then we'll talk about how to defeat it.

The *Dragon of Doubt* breathes fire, but we have the shield of faith. We don't live by logic; we operate by faith. We don't play the victim; we are more than conquerors. We defeat this dragon by not listening to his lies. How do we tune him out? By making sure that the Holy Spirit is the loudest voice in our lives!

The *Dragon of Apathy* lulls men to sleep, but we are dreamers by day. We don't fight fire with fire, and we don't stop sinning by not sinning. We defeat this dragon with a God-given dream that is bigger than fear and better than sin.

The *Dragon of Lust* tells us that more sex, more money, and more applause are what we want, what we need. But lust makes false promises. Instead of fulfilling our desires, lust leaves us feeling empty. We defeat this dragon by standing on God's promises, and no matter how many promises God has made, those promises are *yes* in Christ. So in this isolated instance, being a yes-man is a good thing.

The Dragon of Doubt

I did a chapel for the reigning Super Bowl champions a few years ago, and they let me sit in on their team meeting. The offensive coordinator scripted the first fifteen plays, and I got to watch the game plan play out the next day. The special teams coach spotlighted their opponent's weakness by showing one piece of film over and over again. He scripted a fake field goal, which they actually pulled off in the game!

Think of Scripture as game film. We've got to watch it, study it. We've got to scout the enemy so we know his tendencies. We also have to self-scout so we can overcome our own weaknesses. The enemy disguises his packages and uses different formations, but if we study the film carefully, we will discover that his first trick play is planting seeds of doubt.

> Now the serpent was craftier than any of the wild animals the LORD God had made. He said to the woman, "Did God really say, 'You must not eat from any tree in the garden'?"[15]

The Dragon of Doubt plants seeds of doubt, getting us to second-guess what God has said. He's a liar, but most of those lies aren't bold-faced lies. He's too crafty, too cowardly. Most of his lies are half-truths. And Adam is exhibit A. The enemy exaggerated the restrictions God had placed on Adam. The enemy fooled Adam into thinking that his playground was actually a prison. And he'll do the same thing with our marriages, our jobs, and our churches too!

Doubt is buying into the enemy's lies, believing them to be truth. And if we choose to believe the lie, we're not just buying a bill of goods; we're also calling God a liar!

Is there a lie you've bought into?

When you reverse engineer the first temptation, it's rather obvious that the enemy is trying to get Adam to doubt the goodness of God. That's the chink in the armor. If we doubt His goodness, then we doubt His love, His power, and His grace.

During a recent interview, the archbishop of Canterbury, Justin Welby, was asked what he thought was the chief issue facing the average believer. The archbishop said, "Every Christian I know cannot quite believe that they are loved by God."[16]

I might add one little addendum. We cannot quite believe that God loves us, and we cannot quite believe that God *likes* us. The fact is, God likes you enough to spend all eternity with you.

Jesus encountered the Dragon of Doubt during His forty-day fast in the wilderness. He defended Himself by dropping truth bombs on the devil. Scripture is our double-edged sword. If you want to win the duel with doubt, you have to wield your sword every single day.

Now, let me zoom in on this seed of doubt the enemy planted in Adam. "You must not eat from any tree in the garden. That isn't what God said, is it?" It was only *one tree* that was off-limits! So what the enemy tries to do is make obedience seem harder than it really is. He tries to make it seem impossible, unreasonable.

Resisting temptation isn't easy, that's for sure. And I'll be the first to admit I've lost many battles with pride, lust, greed, and anger. But it's a winnable war. The problem is that most of us feel defeated before the battle even begins. Why? Because we can't imagine winning every battle, every day. After all, who bats a thousand?

This might seem like a Jedi mind trick, but let me ask a question I ask everyone who is struggling with addiction: *Do you think you can win the battle for one day?* By the time a person comes to see me, they're usually battling a habitual sin that seems unbeatable. They feel so defeated that it's tough to even try again. But still, nobody has ever said no to my question.

All you have to do is focus on winning the day! Quit worrying about tomorrow. Don't focus on next week, next month, or next year. Win the day. Leverage today's victory tomorrow. Minimize the losing streaks by not letting bad days turn into bad weeks, bad months, or bad years. Then string some wins together. Before you know it, the momentum will shift and you'll be playing offense again.

The Dragon of Apathy

Let's go ahead and get this out of the way: Eve ate from the Tree of the Knowledge of Good and Evil first. But it wasn't a unilateral decision. Adam was right there. Instead of playing the man, Adam played opossum. He should have stepped up, stepped in. But instead, Adam sat back. Even worse than eating the fruit himself, Adam let Eve eat it, making him an accessory to sin.

> When the woman saw that the fruit of the tree was good for food and pleasing to the eye, and also desirable for gaining

wisdom, she took some and ate it. She also gave some to her husband, who was with her, and he ate it.[17]

The Dragon of Doubt tells us sweet little lies. The Dragon of Apathy lulls us to sleep with a lullaby.

Adam's original sin wasn't eating the forbidden fruit; it was not putting up a fight. "The only thing necessary for the triumph of evil," noted Edmund Burke, "is for good men to do nothing."[18] And that's what Adam did—nothing! Make no mistake about it, indecision *is* a decision and inaction *is* an action. Good things don't happen by default, they happen by design.

The opposite of apathy is response-ability. It's not admitting fault; it's the inability to do nothing. The opposite of apathy is sweat equity. You have to work on your marriage, work on your dream, and work on your faith.

A few weeks after we got married, my wife, Lora, dropped off a dress at the dry cleaners. When she went back to pick it up, the design on her dress went missing. The dry cleaners not only ruined her dress, but they also accused her of lying about it. *Oh, no you didn't!* My wife is the most honest person I have ever known; no one even comes a close second. You can disrespect me and I'll give you a free pass, but if you disrespect my wife, you're going down! I'm pretty laid-back and mild mannered, but that flipped a switch. I went into the dry cleaners like it was the temple and they were money changers! I didn't turn over any tables, but I caused a scene. I'm still not sure if that was the right or wrong thing to do, but I'd do it again. Why? Because no one messes with my wife!

The serpent seduced Eve, and Adam was right by her side. Come on, man. Don't just stand there, do something!

But instead of playing the man, Adam played the passive card. Then when he was confronted by God, he played the passive-aggressive card.

> The woman you put here with me—she gave me some fruit from the tree, and I ate it.[19]

Really? "The woman you put here with me"? Nice try, Adam. Adam blames Eve. Adam blames God. The only person he doesn't think to blame? Himself. Listen, no one wins the blame game. Everybody loses.

Do you have a vision for your marriage? Do you have a strategic plan for parenting?

If your honest answer is no, then you're playing defense instead of offense. And few things are less fulfilling or more frustrating than reactive relationships. You know what your wife wants? A little proactive effort! That's it. And there's a word for it—romance.

Part of playing the man is foreplay, and foreplay doesn't mean four minutes before bed. Foreplay takes forethought. Women can jump-start a man's sexual motor by saying "boo," but most women are more like a Model T Ford with a hand-crank engine. It takes some effort, some intentionality.

The Dragon of Lust

Every red-blooded man battles the Dragon of Lust, and this dragon is disguised as a fair maiden. She promises pleasure, but read the fine print. It'll cost you your integrity—plus tax. The tax is shame!

We think more sex or more money will solve all our problems, but that's dragon-speak. Nothing on this side of heaven will fully satisfy us! As C. S. Lewis observed: "If I find in myself a desire which no experience in this world can satisfy, the most probable explanation is that I was made for another world."[20]

Don't settle for sex.

Don't settle for power.

Don't settle for fame or fortune.

The only thing that will ultimately satisfy our longing for more is more God.

I have a theory: *the answer to every prayer is more of the Holy Spirit*. We want more love, more joy, and more peace, but those are fruits of the Spirit. So what we need is more of the Holy Spirit. And that goes for the rest of the fruit, including the ninth fruit—self-control.

We think forbidden fruit will solve our problems, but it will only complicate them. The only fruit that satisfies is the fruit of the Spirit. Everything we want is the by-product of living a Spirit-led, Spirit-filled life.

One of this dragon's most insidious lies is that God is holding out on you.

> For God knows that when you eat from it your eyes will be opened, and you will be like God, knowing good and evil.[21]

God gave Adam the Garden of Eden *rent-free*! What more could you ask for? You guessed it—one more tree! For the record, there are twenty-three thousand varieties of trees in the world.[22] Thousands of them are fruit trees—orange, almond, cherry, mango, coconut, cashew, and olive, just to name a few. The apple tree alone comes in more than one hundred varieties! My point? Adam could have eaten different fruit from a different tree every day for at least three years! Did he really need one more?

Lust is a lie—a lie that more sex, more food, more power, more applause, or more money will satisfy our wants and needs. It won't. Did you know scientists have coined a term for this? They call it the "hedonic treadmill." When you chase pleasure, you never stop running.

Augustine, who lived quite the hedonistic lifestyle before his encounter with Christ at the age of thirty-one, observed this tendency sixteen centuries ago: "A true saying it is, *Desire hath no rest*, is infinite in itself, endless, and as one calls it, a perpetual rack, or horse-mill."[23]

Horse-mill, treadmill—same difference.

The Dragon of Lust is never satisfied. The more you feed it, the hungrier it gets. Pick a pleasure, any pleasure. It slowly loses its ability to satisfy in the same dose, the same frequency. Over time it takes more and more to satisfy less and less. It's true of success—you're only as good as your last game, your last deal. It's true of money—money might solve some problems, but it creates others. Of course, we all want to test that theory, thinking we'll be the exception to the rule!

Reality check: enough is never enough.

Lust is selfish—it's consumed with getting what it wants. Love is sacrificial—it's consumed with giving what it has.

The only way to meet your deepest needs is by meeting the deepest needs of others! Satisfaction is found on the far side of sacrifice. And that's what playing the man is all about. The Three-Headed Dragon is a daunting foe, but he's a defeated foe. We've got the Father, Son, and Holy Spirit on our side! And if God is for us, who can be against us?

The Toughest Command

Now, let me zero in on marriage for a moment.

I have a theory, and my theory is this: you're selfish. So am I. We all suffer from a sickness called selfishness, and the best antidote is marriage. You can be selfish and married at the same time, but you can't be selfish and *happily* married.

My marital counseling boils down to one piece of advice: *focus on meeting your spouse's needs, not yours.* If you focus on getting your needs met, you will experience perpetual disappointment. If you focus on meeting the needs of your spouse, you will find great fulfillment. Is this easy? No. It's tough love!

I once heard marriage guru Gary Smalley say something so insightful that I've never forgotten it. According to Smalley, most marriages are 80 percent good and 20 percent bad. The only difference between happy and unhappy marriages is where the couple chooses to focus!

If you focus on the 20 percent bad, you'll be unhappy. Now, I'm certainly not suggesting that you ignore the things you or your spouse need to work on. Take responsibility for them. Then work on them. But you cannot afford to forget why you fell in love in the first place. And I'm guessing that has something to do with the 80 percent you should focus on. And you might even want to mention those things to your spouse now and then!

The goal of marriage isn't happiness, it's holiness. And to reach that goal, we must overcome selfishness. So God lets us share a bed, a sink, and a car with someone of the opposite sex.

Absolutely brilliant!

Now, let me add one more thing to the mix.

Marriage helps us overcome our selfishness, but it's not the cure-all. So God gives us children. And if one child doesn't do the trick, God gives us more diapers to change. By the way, *diaper* spelled backwards is *repaid*.

Most of our shortcomings as husbands and fathers can be boiled down to good old-fashioned selfishness. If all our focus is on ourselves, everything else is out of focus. And that brings us back to the tough love. There is no higher standard than this one:

> Husbands, love your wives, just as Christ loved the church and gave himself up for her.[24]

This might be the toughest command in all of Scripture. In fact, I don't think it's attainable by mortal men. But that's the standard Jesus set, so that's what we shoot for.

Hide-and-Seek

Remember Adam's original reaction after his original sin? He hid from the All-Seeing Eye. Can't you picture Adam hiding behind a sapling, his body sticking out on both sides? It'd be comedy if it weren't a tragedy!

God knew right where Adam was, yet He called out, "Where are you?" The question is, why? I think God was giving Adam an opportunity to be found, to be forgiven. It was a grace period. And Adam's explanation?

> I heard you in the garden, and I was afraid because I was naked; so I hid.[25]

Afraid?
Afraid of what?

Afraid of the God who loves you perfectly and forgives you freely?

For the first time, Adam felt fear. Then he let fear dictate his decisions. The sad irony is that Adam was afraid of the only One who could help him and heal him. It's as illogical as a fear of doctors when you get sick.

Most of us are imprisoned by one or two or three mistakes we've made in our past. We know that we're forgiven by God because we've confessed our sin. But we can't seem to forgive ourselves. The key, in my opinion, is confessing our sin to someone else. Until we do, that secret sin blackmails us. But once we confess it to someone else, shame loses its grip!

John Donne was considered by many to be the greatest poet of his generation. Donne went to Oxford when he was eleven years old and went on to serve as the dean of St. Paul's Cathedral in London. He was übersuccessful by every external standard, but he lived in a state of shame because of a secret sin. Before his conversion to Christ, Donne had composed obscene poetry for the woman he had secretly married. That secret kept Donne locked up inside.

Like Donne, many of us are held hostage by a secret sin. And the enemy wants to blackmail us! His secret weapon is getting us to keep our secret sin a secret. But secret sin is like kryptonite—it drains us of the raw passion we need to play the man. We think we'll die if our sin is discovered, but the truth is, we'll come to life!

Quit pretending to be perfect.

Quit acting as if everything is okay.

It takes moral courage to come clean and confess your sin, but it's a deathblow to the Three-Headed Dragon.

Play the man!

5

Sockdolager

The Fifth Virtue of Manhood:
True Grit

Fill the earth and subdue it.

—Genesis 1:28

May 24, 1869
The Colorado River

In 1869, a thirty-five-year-old professor of geology named
John Wesley Powell attempted something thought to be impossible. In fact, experts called it a death wish. In the mid-
nineteenth century, there was a blank spot on the map of
America that was as mysterious as the Bermuda Triangle and
as big as any state in the union.[1] Mapmakers inscribed the
word *unexplored* on that part of the map to fill in the blank.

To the average westward emigrant, it was a caution sign to steer clear. To John Wesley Powell, it was his beck and call.

Powell's dream was to be the first person to cross the Grand Canyon by traversing the Colorado River. The catch is that neither Powell nor any member of his nine-man crew had ever run a single rapid. If they had known up front that they would encounter five hundred rapids over a thousand-mile stretch of river, it's doubtful whether they would have attempted it. What they did know before embarking is that it was an all-or-nothing, do-or-die mission. Once you enter the canyon, the only exit is out the other side!

Powell stood five feet, six and a half inches tall and weighed one hundred and twenty pounds soaking wet. There is one other noteworthy fact—Powell had lost his right arm in the Civil War. So the man leading the flotilla of flatbed boats down the Colorado River could not row, bail, or swim.

What's your excuse for not going after your goal?

The editor of the *Springfield Republican*, Samuel Bowles, met Powell shortly before his expedition. Bowles warned, "Whoever dares to venture into this canyon will never come out alive."[2] Bowles thought it was foolhardy, but he admired Powell's willingness to try. Or more accurately, his unwillingness to *not* try!

Navigating the river is so difficult and dangerous that up until World War II, only 250 people had done it. Based on today's rules and regulations, Powell wouldn't even qualify for a permit. But Powell wasn't a man to let limitations get in the way of his goal. One biographer described Powell as being "as single-minded as a buzz saw."[3] And that's what it takes to accomplish the impossible—a single-minded stick-to-itiveness come hell or high water. In a word: *grit*. Even better, true grit.

That's is the fifth virtue of manhood. It's resilience in the face of rejection, fortitude in the face of fear. It's a no guts, no glory approach to life, even in the face of impossible odds.

I certainly believe in the power of prayer. We must *pray like it depends on God*. But I also believe that a good old-fashioned work ethic honors God too. So you have to *work like it depends on you*. "You supply the grit," said the old Welsh preacher, "and God will supply the grace."[4]

The Ultimate Rapid

One of the most exhilarating weeks of my life was spent rafting the Colorado River with my youngest son, Josiah. Unlike Powell, our group had guides and a map! That rafting adventure was Josiah's Rite of Passage at the end of his Year of Discipleship. The July temperatures averaged a scorching 108 degrees, but the river was a bone-chilling 48 degrees. That'll cool you off in a New York minute.

At one point we held a little contest among some of the men on the trip to see who could stay under the water the longest. In a heated pool I can hold my breath for at least sixty seconds. I lasted only twenty seconds in the Colorado River before getting a brain freeze! But that was longer than any of the other guys, so I had bragging rights the rest of the trip.

For five days we ran rapids, slept under stars, and explored side canyons. We bodysurfed the Little Colorado, climbed cliffs I didn't think were scalable, and hiked out of the Grand Canyon itself. All of those experiences were epic, but the hands-down highlight was a class 7 rapid called Sockdolager.[5]

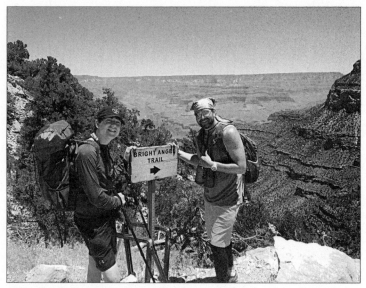

Josiah and Mark are all smiles as they begin their trek on the Bright Angel Trail.

If you look up *sockdolager* in the dictionary, it means "knockout blow."[6] And that's exactly what the rapid felt like—a 48-degree punch in the face. As we approached the rapid, my adrenaline was pumping like pregame warm-ups. We white-knuckled the handles of the raft and held on for dear life. Breaking through the rapid reminded me of running through the human-sized Hula-Hoop signs our cheerleaders used to make for our basketball team in high school. As we broke through the rapid, Josiah yelled at the top of his mid-puberty voice, "We are men! We are men!"

That will forever rank as one of the greatest moments of my life.

Remember Hannibal's famous line from the TV show *A-Team*? "I love it when a plan comes together." This was exactly that—a plan coming together. My goal in planning that Rite of Passage trip was to draw a line of demarcation between boyhood and manhood. Mission accomplished at mile marker 79.1 on the Colorado River. Josiah crossed a threshold, and we did it together.

I've since wondered: *What was it that gave Josiah such a sense of manliness in that moment?* I think part of it was the fact that he faced his fears and fought through them. Doing something dangerous and difficult certainly contributed. And another piece of the puzzle is the fact that our guides pushed us past our perceived physical limits. It all added up to a feeling of manliness!

I'm more and more convinced that men need *an element of danger*. It's one way we come alive. It's one way we discover who we really are. Without danger, our sense of manliness atrophies. We become like caged animals. If there isn't a healthy and holy outlet for our testosterone, we often find unhealthy and unholy outlets.

Let me ask a question: When have you felt most like a man?

I haven't done a quantitative study on the subject, but I have a hunch. If you're anything like me, you feel most like a man when you're pushed to your limits and beyond. That's how I felt when I reached the South Rim of the Grand Canyon and looked back at the nearly ten-mile-long Bright Angel Trail we had conquered.

I'm not getting any younger, so hiking isn't getting any easier. Plus, I had chronic asthma and two knees that have been surgically reconstructed because of ACL injuries. It wasn't easy ascending a vertical mile, but that is precisely what made it memorable.

Leading up to that trip, I had gotten a little lazy. It had been a few years since I had tested my physical limits. That's how

I discovered, or rediscovered, that I feel most like a man when I'm in a situation that demands everything I have to give.

A decade ago, I was part of a mission team that built a mud hut in Ethiopia. It was like Habitat for Humanity—Ethiopian style! We actually mixed the mud and hay with our feet. It was like doing a stair-stepper in quicksand. My quads were on fire after a few minutes, and it took most of the day! I don't think I've ever been more physically exhausted than I was at the end of that day, or more covered in mud. But I felt like a man. Why? Because I tested the limits of my strength, and I did it in pursuit of a kingdom cause. We put a roof over the head of a precious Ethiopian grandmother named Lulit. As I fell asleep that night, I felt like it was as close as I've ever come to loving God with all of my strength.

Do Hard Things

When you hike the Grand Canyon or build a mud hut, you discover muscles you didn't know you had. And that's precisely the point. You've got to put yourself in positions that will push you past your previous limits. That's how you grow.

"What does not kill me," said Friedrich Nietzsche, "strengthens me."[7] Or if you prefer Kelly Clarkson's hit single "Stronger": "What doesn't kill you makes you stronger, stand a little taller."[8]

The way you gain strength is by breaking down your muscle fibers. Then, with the help of protein, those muscle fibers grow back even stronger. What's true physically is true emotionally and spiritually. When you go through a season of stress, think of it as an emotional workout. It might feel like a breakdown, but God is building up your emotional fortitude! Maybe it's time to set a stretch goal.

We must choose to do things that push us past our previous limits. About the time I released my first book, *In a Pit with a Lion on a Snowy Day*, my publisher released a book by two teenagers titled *Do Hard Things: A Teenage Rebellion against Low Expectations*. It was one of the twelve titles I assigned during my son Parker's Year of Discipleship. And we didn't just read the book; we put it into practice by training for a sprint triathlon for his *physical challenge*. A 10K race would have been easier, but I wanted a stretch goal. I wanted to push Parker to tap his potential by attempting something I wasn't sure he was capable of. The running and biking portion of the triathlon didn't concern me, but I knew that the open ocean swim would challenge both of us.

The day of the race, the swim portion was almost canceled because the ocean waves crested at more than six feet high. We probably drank a gallon of salt water and resorted to the doggy paddle a time or two, but crossing that finish line gave us a sense of unparalleled fulfillment.

My point? Do hard things. It's part and parcel of playing the man.

Work hard. Play hard. Pray hard.

East of Eden

John Wesley Powell and his crew weren't cut out for desk jobs—civilian life was too civil. Powell heard the call of the wild, and he responded to wanderlust. In his younger years, before he lost his arm in battle, Powell rowed the length of the Mississippi River! He also conquered the Ohio, Illinois, and Des Moines Rivers.

What drove Powell to row those rivers? What drove him to attempt an even more difficult and dangerous challenge after having lost an arm? In my opinion, it was an ancient instinct, an instinct that is as old as Eden itself.

> God blessed them and said to them, "Be fruitful and increase in number; fill the earth and subdue it."[9]

People often assume Adam and Eve would have remained in the Garden of Eden forever if they had not eaten from the Tree of the Knowledge of Good and Evil, but that is a mistaken notion. Long before the fall, God told them to fill the earth and subdue it. It was an invitation to explore. I call it the Genesis Commission.

Perhaps Powell was responding to this ancient instinct, responding to this ancient calling. At the time, the Grand Canyon was unexplored and people knew very little about it, which Powell saw as an embarrassment to America. "Is any other nation so ignorant of itself?"[10] he asked. So he set out to subdue the mystery of one of the world's natural wonders. Perhaps that's how Adam felt. After all, everything east of Eden was *unexplored*.

Adam could have traveled 24,901 miles in any direction and never have seen the same landscape twice. He had 196,940,000 square miles of uncharted territory to explore.[11] Not unlike John Wesley Powell, who navigated through unexplored parts of America, Adam was commissioned to explore planet Earth.

In the grand scheme of things, the astronomer who charts the stars, the geneticist who maps the human genome, the oceanographer who explores the barrier reef, the ornithologist who preserves endangered bird species, the physicist who pulls on the string theory, and the chemist who charts molecular structures all have one thing in common. They are all explorers. Whether they know it or not, each one is fulfilling the call to subdue in their own unique way.

Kabash!

To conquer or be conquered, that is the question.

The word *subdue* comes from the Hebrew word *kabash*. It sounds like a Batman fight word, doesn't it? *BAM! WHAM! KAPOW! KABASH!* And its meaning isn't far from that. Picture a submission move in mixed martial arts. Kabash is an arm bar, a choke hold.

When you go to the gym, you are subduing your body. Whether it's the bench press or leg press, you're making those weights submit to your muscles. The same is true of running a marathon or rowing a river. At its core, *kabash* is pushing the limits of what you're capable of. That's how you discover new capacities within yourself. It's also how you come alive in new ways.

Here are a few core aspects of *kabash*:

1. *To make a path*

    It's Robert Frost standing at the place where the proverbial road diverged.[12] *Kabash* is taking the road less traveled. It's blazing a trail and leaving a path behind so that others can follow in your footsteps.

2. *To bring under control*

    It's cowboys breaking a new colt.

It's farmers plowing a field for planting.

It's songwriters combining notes and lyrics to make music.

3. *To conquer*

When we hiked the Grand Canyon from rim to rim, I felt like we were subduing it one step at a time. We conquered the Grand Canyon. I felt the same way when we made the four-day trek to Machu Picchu and when we summited Half Dome.

We are called to conquer. In fact, we are "more than conquerors" through Christ.[13] Of course, the hardest thing to conquer isn't nature—it's human nature. It's conquering the sin nature in me. According to King Solomon, it's harder than, better than, conquering a city![14]

Wage War

On Halloween night in 1900, a ten-year-old boy named Ike wanted to go trick-or-treating with his older brothers. When his parents told him he was too young, Ike flew into an uncontrollable rage. He ran out the front door and punched an apple tree until his knuckles were raw and red from blood.[15]

Ike's father lashed him with a hickory stick and sent him to his room. He was still sobbing in his pillow an hour later when his mother walked into his room and sat down in a rocking chair next to his bed. Ida Eisenhower was the oracle of the family, repeating maxims like, "God deals the cards, and we play them." In this instance, she cited Proverbs 16:32:

He that conquereth his soul is greater than he that taketh a city.

At seventy-six, as Ike surveyed the landscape of his life, he identified this one moment as a moment that made all the difference in the world.

"I have always looked back on that conversation as one of the most valuable moments in my life. To my youthful mind, it seemed like she talked for hours, but I suppose the whole affair was ended in fifteen or twenty minutes."[16]

Ike Eisenhower would grow up to serve two terms as president of the United States. But his greatest contribution to this country, to the world, came as supreme allied commander during Operation Overlord—the liberation of France and invasion of Germany that began on the beaches of Normandy on June 6, 1944.

Self-control didn't come naturally to Eisenhower. In fact, he ranked 125 out of 164 for discipline in his graduating class at West Point.[17] And according to Ida, of all his siblings, he had the most to learn about controlling his passions. As she bandaged his bleeding hands after beating on that apple tree, she warned him that anger only injures the person who harbors it.

Long before the supreme allied commander could lead the most powerful army the world had ever seen to defeat the Axis Powers, a ten-year-old boy had to learn how to conquer his own soul. That was an inciting incident, and that Proverb became the script of Eisenhower's life.

If we don't conquer our own soul, we sinfully subdue as an act of selfishness. In fact, the word *kabash* can mean "to molest." It can be a misuse of the strength God has given us as men—a sinful expression of subduing. Playing the man starts with subduing the sin nature inside of us. Then we subdue as an act of stewardship.

So how do we conquer our own souls?

We take every thought captive and make it obedient to Christ.[18]

We make a covenant with our eyes.[19]

We take up our cross daily and deny ourselves.[20]

We discipline our bodies.[21]

We crucify the desires of the flesh.[22]

These things are easier said than done, but they are possible.

We have to wage war with the sin nature. And in my experience, the best tactic is blockading the sin nature by cutting off supply lines. We have to starve lust to death. And that goes for greed and pride too. That's the only way to win the war with the sin nature. And we have to wage war every single day!

One more Eisenhower anecdote. While a student at West Point, Ike was a four-pack-a-day smoker. Then one day he quit cold turkey. How?

"I simply gave myself an order," he said.[23]

Is there an executive order you need to give yourself?

I don't know what you need to quit, but whatever it is, try issuing an order. If you don't master lust, lust will master you. And the same goes for pride, greed, and anger. Whether it's looking at pornography, losing your temper, or cutting corners on your tax return, stop it.

In the book of Revelation, God gives high praise to the church at Thyatira for their love, faith, and perseverance. But then He levels an accusation against the sin of toleration:

Nevertheless, I have this against you: You tolerate that woman Jezebel, who calls herself a prophet. By her teaching she misleads my servants into sexual immorality and the eating of food sacrificed to idols.[24]

Sexual indiscretion was being tolerated. And whatever we tolerate will eventually dominate us. All the enemy wants and needs is a foothold. Over time, that little compromise will grow into a big problem.

Is there something in your life that you are tolerating? Give yourself an order to stop!

Say Not

The hardest part of the body to subdue is the tongue.[25] Well, perhaps the second hardest! So let me issue a gentleman's challenge. What we refer to as locker room talk, the Bible calls sin.

Nor should there be obscenity, foolish talk or coarse joking, which are out of place.[26]

Here's a simple rule of thumb: *don't say something about someone that you wouldn't say if they were standing there.* And above all, honor your wife with your words. If you're going to talk about her behind her back, make sure you're bragging!

There is a powerful little phrase repeated in Scripture: "say not."

Whatever you verbalize, you give power to. When you voice negative thoughts, you're reinforcing what's wrong. Over time, it often becomes a self-fulfilling prophecy.

Instead of verbalizing negativity, speak words of faith. Instead of verbalizing complaints, speak words of praise.

When God called Jeremiah to be a prophet, Jeremiah felt overwhelmed and underqualified. He used inexperience as an excuse, and God rebuked his excuse.

Say not, I am a child.[27]

Quit making excuses!

I'm too old. I'm too young. I had bad parents. I've made too many mistakes. I don't have the education. I don't have the experience.

Say not!

What needs to go on your "say not" list? You can start with obscenities, foolish talk, and coarse joking. While you're at it, add gossiping and lying. And to top it off, quit insulting others or bragging about yourself.

If we can subdue our tongues, there is no part of our bodies we cannot control. James likened the tongue to the rudder of a boat—it turns the whole ship.

When we put bits into the mouths of horses to make them obey us, we can turn the whole animal. Or take ships as an example. Although they are so large and are driven by strong winds, they are steered by a very small rudder wherever the pilot wants to go. Likewise, the tongue is a small part of the body, but it makes great boasts.[28]

The Resilient Ones

When the reality TV show *Survivor* first debuted, I was an avid viewer. At the end of each episode, an immunity challenge was given, which was designed to test the physical, emotional, and intellectual limits of contestants. The weekly winner earned immunity so he or she couldn't be voted out of the tribe and off the show.

My all-time favorite immunity challenge tested grit. In keeping with the motto of the show, it was designed to see who could outlast the others in a war of wills. All ten survivors stood on top of totem poles surrounded by water. Whenever a contestant fell off the pole by losing their balance or losing their patience, they were disqualified. The competition lasted much longer than anyone expected. Through the dark hours of the night, three very tired, very cold competitors were still standing. The winner lasted ten hours and eighteen minutes!

What kept them on top of the totem pole? True grit.

The word *toughness*, when referring to metal, is a measure of how much it can deform without fracturing. In other words, it's the ability to bend without breaking. The toughest metals can withstand stress and strain because of their resiliency.

Metal toughness and mental toughness are similar.

Grit is the place where passion and perseverance meet.

Grit is an attitude—an unwillingness to give up, to give in.

Grit is a sanctified stubborn streak! [29]

Even if you're hanging on by a thread, you hang in there. No matter how many times you've been knocked down, you get back up! You keep on keeping on no matter what, no matter when, no matter how.

In his brilliant book *A Resilient Life*, Gordon MacDonald says, "In the great race of life, there are some Christ-followers who stand out from all the rest. I call them the resilient ones. The further they run, the stronger they get."[30]

The Blood Round

I have a friend, Chris Owen, whose son Ethan finished his freshman year of wrestling at Southeastern University with an incredible 40–6 record. In fact, Ethan came within one match of becoming an all-American. In wrestling circles, that final round is called the blood round—win and you're in, lose and you're out.

It's winner takes all, all-American.

In the Bible, Jacob's all-night wrestling match with God might be the best picture of true grit. Jacob refused to let go until God blessed him. That one act of grit changed his identity, changed his destiny.[31]

He was no longer Jacob the deceiver. He was Israel, "he who struggles with God."

Jacob won the blood round. So did Jesus.

When Jesus was praying in the Garden of Gethsemane on the night of His betrayal, Scripture says His "sweat was like drops of blood."[32] At His crucifixion, His back was bloodied with a Roman flagrum. Blood trickled into His eyes from the crown of thorns. Blood oozed out of His hands and feet as they were pierced with seven-inch nails. And blood gushed from His side, which was impaled by a Roman spear.

It was a bloody affair, but Jesus won the blood round. How did He endure the cross, scorning its shame? The short answer is true grit infused with amazing grace.

For the joy set before him he endured the cross.[33]

Jesus endured the pain of the cross by fixing his eyes on us—the joy of His salvation. When He was on the cross, we were on his mind. And the way we stay strong in the face of pain and suffering and trials is by fixing our eyes on Him!

> Therefore, since we are surrounded by such a great cloud of witnesses, let us throw off everything that hinders and the sin that so easily entangles. And let us run with perseverance the race marked out for us, fixing our eyes on Jesus, the author and perfecter of our faith.[34]

We have a cloud of witnesses cheering us on, and that gets the adrenaline pumping! But best of all, Jesus Himself is at the finish line waiting for us. That's our second wind. If He hung on the cross for us, we can carry our cross for Him!

Team Sport

On May 6, 1954, a British medical student named Roger Bannister became the first person to run a mile in less than four minutes. Bannister was immortalized, but he couldn't have done it without two friends who paced him—Chris Chataway and Chris Basher.[35] Few people know their names, but without those pacemakers, Bannister wouldn't have broken the record.

Grit is a team sport.

You can endure almost anything if you don't have to endure it alone! Enter Jesus. He's the friend who sticks closer than a brother. But we also need a band of brothers during tough times. They lessen the load on our shoulders during tough times, and they multiply the joy in our hearts during good times!

I don't think Jonathan would have or could have scaled the pass at Mikmash, scoring a decisive victory against the

Philistines, without his armor-bearer.[36] We live in an individualistic society that applauds the lone wolf, but we all need a pack.

Who are your pacemakers?

And who are you pacing?

When I put together my first life goal list, almost all of my goals could be accomplished by me, myself, and I. Then I ran that triathlon with Parker and realized it was twice as joyous crossing the finish line together! So I went back and added a relational component to most of my goals.

The Bible says that bad company corrupts good character, but let me flip the script. Good company helps us go from good to great. You'll never achieve your true potential by yourself. You need friends who will pace you and push you. After all, iron sharpens iron!

Without his crew, John Wesley Powell never would have accomplished his goals. There were a thousand things he couldn't do with one arm! Powell may have been the lead actor, but he had a supporting cast that rowed, bailed, and portaged. And for the record, they saved his life more than once!

One of my favorite stories about Powell is his lifelong friendship with Mississippi congressman C. E. Hooker. Powell lost his right arm fighting for the Union, while Hooker lost his left arm fighting for the Confederacy. They were wartime enemies who became friends via a unique pact. Whenever either of them bought a new pair of gloves, he would send the other the extra glove he couldn't use! For thirty years, they exchanged gloves as a token of friendship.[37]

Don't Settle Down

True grit was cultivated in John Wesley Powell at an early age. By the time he turned twelve, he was plowing and planting his family's sixty-acre farm, then hauling the crops to market and selling them.

That'll make a man of you in a hurry!

His grit was tested when his right arm was shot off during the Battle of Shiloh. Three out of four surgical operations during the Civil War were amputations, and battlefield surgeons performed so many of them that they could remove a limb in six minutes flat.[38] Of course, they did so without adequate anesthetics or analgesics! For the rest of his life, Powell felt pain in the raw nerve endings where his injury occurred.[39] But that didn't keep him from returning to battle just months after losing his arm!

A few blocks from where I live on Capitol Hill, Powell's journal of his trip down the Colorado River is housed at the National Museum of Natural History. It's like a message in a bottle, complete with 150-year-old watermarks. Part of what makes the journal so valuable is the fact that it took a quantum effort for Powell to record his thoughts in writing. After losing his dominant arm, he had to teach himself how to write with his weak hand. And to further complicate matters, he didn't have a second hand to hold the paper steady or to keep it from blowing away as winds blew through the canyon. Powell chased down the pages of his journal more than once! So the paper trail Powell left from that trip came only through great effort.

Before Powell set out on his grand adventure, his father tried to stop him. "Wes, you are a maimed man," his dad told him. "Settle down at teaching. It is a noble profession. Get this nonsense of science and adventure out of your mind."[40]

My advice? Don't settle down! When the going gets tough, the tough get going. It's never too late to be who you might have been.

It takes tremendous grit to go after your dreams. It takes tremendous grit to fight for your marriage. It takes tremendous grit to be a true friend, a true father. But that is precisely the point.

It takes a man.

It makes a man.

Play the man!

6

Born for the Storm

The Sixth Virtue of Manhood: Clear Vision

Your young men will see visions, your old men will dream dreams.

—Acts 2:17

New Orleans, Louisiana
January 8, 1815

During the War of 1812, General Andrew Jackson marched more than two thousand Tennessee volunteers from Nashville to New Orleans. With bravado they fought the decisive Battle of New Orleans. The sad irony is that the battle was unnecessary because the war had already ended, but it took two weeks for news of the peace treaty to cross the Atlantic!

119

The fighting took its toll on Jackson's troops, but sickness proved to be the deadiest and most dangerous enemy. One hundred fifty soldiers became gravely ill, fifty-six of whom could not even stand.

Dr. Samuel Hogg asked the general what he wanted him to do. "To do, sir?" Jackson answered. "You are to leave not a man on the ground."[1] It wasn't official code of conduct yet, but Jackson embodied the military motto "Leave no man behind."

Andrew Jackson ordered his officers to give up their horses to those who were sick, and the general was the first to do so. Jackson marched 531 miles on foot. Somewhere between New Orleans and Nashville, he earned the nickname "Old Hickory," the same name under which he would campaign for president fifteen years later.

Before winning the White House, the seventh president of the United States is alleged to have fought as many as thirteen duels, which explains the thirty-seven pistols in his gun collection. I'm not advocating the reintroduction of dueling, but it does reveal something about Jackson's character—Old Hickory wasn't one to shrink from a fight, especially when honor was at stake!

"I was born for the storm," said Jackson. "And the calm does not suit me."[2] When the sea is calm, no one needs a sailor! Anyone can captain the ship in that situation. But when a perfect storm threatens to capsize your marriage or drown your dreams, you must play the man. A true man doesn't sit back. He steps up and steps in. He fights the good fight, even when it seems like all is lost. Why? Because a true man is born for the storm.

Don't man overboard.

Man the oars!

The Gospels recount a terrible storm that swept across the Sea of Galilee, threatening to capsize a boat carrying Jesus and His disciples. Somehow Jesus was sound asleep in the stern. The disciples, some of whom were seasoned sailors, were scared stiff. Then Jesus woke up, stood up, and rebuked the wind and the waves, and the sea became calm!

What storm do you need to rebuke?

What situation is begging you to stand up and say, "Peace, be still"?

Jesus rebuked the wind and waves. He also rebuked fevers and Pharisees, demons and disease. And He rebuked them with remarkably few words.

How did He do it? He understood the authority that was His as the Son of God, the same authority we have as the sons of God.

Why did He do it? Because He understood His mission. It's not insignificant that Jesus went on a type of vision quest right before changing career tracks from carpentry to ministry. Nothing will give you crystal clear vision like forty days of fasting in the wilderness! And that's the sixth virtue of manhood—*clear vision.*

Jesus emerged from the wilderness with a laser-focused mission statement. Afterward, at the synagogue in Nazareth, He read from the scroll of Isaiah:

> The Spirit of the Lord is on me, because he has anointed me to proclaim good news to the poor. He has sent me to proclaim freedom for the prisoners and recovery of sight for the blind, to set the oppressed free, and to proclaim the year of the Lord's favor.[3]

When He finished, He rolled up the scroll and rolled up His sleeves before announcing: "Today this scripture is fulfilled in your hearing."[4]

Drop the mic!

Jesus was a man on a mission; He had a clear vision. You can't play the man without a vision any more than you can play piano without a piano or play football without a football.

Do you have a mission statement for your life?

What about a vision statement for your marriage?

How about core values for your family?

Or what about life goals or a life plan?

Men need something to fight for, something to fight against. It's how we survive the storms that are bound to batter us now and then. Without a vision, a man will waste his life away. But with a clear vision, he's a force to be reckoned with.

The Self-Made Man

Andrew Jackson revered his mother, Elizabeth Jackson. "There was never a woman like her," said Jackson. "She was gentle as a dove and brave as a lioness." And her last words would echo in his life forever. Jackson said, "Her last words have been the law of my life."[5]

In her last conversation with Andrew, Elizabeth said, "If I should not see you again, I wish you to remember and treasure up some things I have already said to you: in this world you will have to make your own way. To do that you must have friends."[6]

Let me drill down on that piece of advice, because it's too important to pass over: *you must have friends.*

In the nineteenth century, the concept of the self-made man was canonized. But the truth is, there are no self-made men! We all need a circle of friends, a band of brothers. More often than not, we become the composite of the people we surround ourselves with. So choose your friends wisely!

In the beginning, God said, "It is not good for man to be alone."[7]

Nothing has changed. It's still not good for man to be alone. Eve was one solution to the problem, but she wasn't the only solution. Every man needs a friend in the same way David needed Jonathan and Jonathan needed David.

Have you ever been on the bench press and come to the realization that you've attempted one rep too many? There is no way you can lift it off your chest one more time, so you have to tilt the bar or roll it down your body. I've been in that embarrassing situation a time or two.

You need a spotter!

It's as true in everyday life as it is at the gym.

For the past two decades, one of my spotters has been Dick Foth. As a rookie pastor, I needed someone to help me navigate ministry. And to be honest, I needed someone to help me navigate marriage too! Dick had been there and done that. Dick and his wife, Ruth, have celebrated more than fifty anniversaries. And he's been ordained for more than half a century now. In other words, he's been playing the man longer than I've been alive. Just as my parents passed along their DNA, Dick has passed along his wisdom. I wouldn't be who I am or where I am without him. I used to call Dick a *mentor*, and then I apologized to him. He's more than that—he's a spiritual father. I need him, and strangely, he needs me.

Why? Because friendship isn't optional. And ideally, some of those friendships will be intergenerational.

Every Timothy needs a Paul—a spiritual father.

Every Paul needs a Timothy—a spiritual son.

And we all need a Barnabas—a spiritual brother.

Sustain Your Manhood

At the end of her last will and testament, Elizabeth Jackson challenged her son with a unique exhortation: "Sustain your manhood always."[8]

Over time it's easy for men to become emasculated emotionally. We make so many mistakes that we stop forgiving ourselves! Or we get so discouraged with our dream that we give up on it. We quit trying to win the battle with temptation; we quit trying to woo our wives; we quit trying to father our children.

Men, we quit too quickly, too easily.

Sustain your manhood!

Besides the Bible, which Andrew Jackson read three chapters from every day, no book had a greater influence on his psyche than *The Scottish Chiefs*. "I have always thought that William Wallace, as a virtuous patriot and warrior, was the best model for a young man."[9] What was it about Braveheart that Jackson admired? Wallace embodied what Jackson called "stubborn virtue."[10]

When I first got married, my stubborn streak led to many "marital conversations." God wants to crucify the selfish stubborn streak in all of us, but then He wants to resurrect it and use it for His purposes. I call it a sanctified stubborn streak. Playing the man is refusing to cower in the face of challenging circumstances. It's facing your fears and demons. It's playing the hand you've been dealt, even if you don't like your cards. And even when it's tough to keep a promise, playing the man means being a promise keeper. Or to take it one step further—it's being a promise proclaimer.

Stand fast in the faith, quit you like men, be strong.[11]

Some translations say "act like men," but I like "quit you like men." To quit yourself like a man means you don't quit—it's the epitome of perseverance. The Greek word here, *andrizomai*, literally means "to play the man." It's possessing qualities befitting a man—the virtues of manhood.

I often tell fellow pastors, "Don't focus on church growth; focus on personal growth." If you grow yourself, everyone around you will grow because of it. And that goes for any occupation or any situation. Grow yourself and you'll grow your platform, grow your network.

Playing the man means not playing the comparison game. Everyone loses at that game. Focus on strengthening yourself little by little. You be the best *you* that you can be.

This reminds me of David. One of the low points in his life was the day he discovered the Amalekites had raided Ziglag and taken all the women and children captive. David's men talked of stoning him. David was greatly distressed, but he sustained his manhood. How?

David strenghtened himself in the LORD his God.[12]

If you forget who God is, you forget who you are! And the fallout is self-doubt. The way you strengthen yourself in the

Lord is by reminding yourself of who God is and what He has done. God is *the* Promise Keeper! You stand fast in the faith by standing on the promises of God.

Like every parent, I've made lots of mistakes. But one thing I've done right is praying the promises of God for my kids When they were young, I turned Luke 2:52 into a daily prayer: "May you grow in wisdom and stature, and in favor with God and with man." I've prayed that prayer and proclaimed that promise thousands of times.

Playing the man means proclaiming the promises of God.

Playing the man means proclaiming the praises of God.

A Man on a Mission

I love the classic scene from *The Blues Brothers* when Elwood Blues announces: "We're on a mission from God."[13] I also love the backflips that his brother does down the center aisle of the church. What a great way to go to the altar!

It's a mission from God that keeps us on the straight and narrow. When we are busy with the Father's business, we can't be sidetracked. A mission from God not only motivates us to do the right thing, it also demotivates us from doing the wrong thing.

If you aren't on a mission from God, you aren't really living—you're dying. You aren't just wasting your God-given potential, you're wasting space. You're dead weight.

I have a theory.

When a church loses sight of their mission, they involuntarily and unwittingly create problems to keep themselves busy! Before you know it, they're *playing church* instead of being the church. Instead of advancing the kingdom, they're

126

advancing their program. Instead of exercising their authority, they're advocating their agenda. And instead of the church advancing, it's taken off course by sideways energy!

The same goes for men.

The first-century church had issues, just like the church does today, but they were full steam ahead.

> From the days of John the Baptist until now the kingdom of heaven suffers violence, and violent men take it by force.[14]

The Danish philosopher and theologian Søren Kierkegaard believed that boredom was the root of all evil. I absolutely concur. Boredom spells trouble.

When men get bored, they do dumb stuff. Remember David? He should have been on the battlefield with his army, not on a roof deck spying on Bathsheba. He wasn't getting his adrenaline rush from battle, so he found another outlet.

Boredom is often the first sign of sin. So my advice is this: stay busy! Not busy as in busybody or busy as in workaholic. A fine line can be drawn between a healthy work ethic and work becoming the idol where you find your identity. Keep busy with the Father's business.

Simply put, follow Jesus.

If you do, you'll be anything but bored.

I've said it before, but let me say it again: you don't not sin by not sinning. You need a vision that is bigger and better than sin. You need a mission that demands every second of your time, every ounce of your talent, and every penny of your treasure. Then you won't waste it on lesser things.

I've grown to love and respect a group of men from Calvary Church in Naperville, Illinois—the church I grew up in, the church my father-in-law pastored for thirty-one years. They're ordinary men with ordinary names—Ed, Keith, Steve, Pete, Troy, Vern, Tom, Jerry, Fred, Dan, and Mark. They have strong backs, calloused hands, and a clear vision from God. Together they've taken dozens of mission trips, helping build the kingdom by building things, including our first office space at National Community Church, as well as our DC Dream Center.

You name it and they can build it. Why do these men use their vacation time to serve others? Why do they do it on their own dime? Because they're on a mission from God.

You can't be around this band of brothers for five minutes without being blessed. But along with blessing others, serving has kept them busy. And they are better men because of it.

Vision Retreat

When I first decided to craft a Discipleship Covenant and embark on a Year of Discipleship, I had no curriculum. In fact, I had no clue! Sure, I had read a few books on the subject. But it was DIY—do it yourself. And while I hope this book gives you some ideas to adopt, you'll also need to adapt those ideas to your children, to your situation.

One of the best things about discipling others is that it teaches you self-discipline. You think you're doing it for your children, but you might be the primary beneficiary! Why? Because it forces you to figure out what it means to play the man.

Several years after getting married and starting our family, I came to the painful realization that I had a vision for the church I pastor, but I didn't really have a vision for our family. It's hard to imagine a business succeeding without a vision or without values, much less a family! So I began to brainstorm with my oldest son what values we wanted to define us as Battersons. And, yes, I included my wife in the process too! I wanted values that everybody in the family could own so that these values could own us.

When we started, our family had a few mantras that we repeated often.

Choose your battles wisely.
Fess up when you mess up.
Your focus determines your reality.
If you drop your keys in a river of molten lava, let 'em go, man, 'cause they're gone!

Yes, that last one is a Jack Handey "Deep Thought." And, yes, it doubled as a Batterson family value! As you can see, we desperately needed some values that were more than deep thoughts. We wanted timeless words that would define who we are and who we wanted to become. And we landed on four of them: *humility*, *gratitude*, *generosity*, and *courage*.

If you've never crafted a family vision statement or identified family values, here are five simple steps that will help you get started:

1. *Start with prayer.* The way you get a vision from God is by getting into His presence. So don't just brainstorm, praystorm! The process of identifying vision and values always begins by aligning yourself with God. If you want a word *from* God, then get into the Word *of* God. As you prayerfully read Scripture, the Holy Spirit will quicken words and verses. When He does, journal them. Then circle those words and verses in prayer.

2. *Do your homework.* Vision doesn't materialize out of thin air. Read anything and everything you can get your hands on. Books, especially biographies, are the seedbed of vision. But don't stop there. Read some books with skin on them. Whose marriage do you genuinely admire? Which parents do you greatly respect? Take them out to dinner and ask many questions. Then adopt and adapt those ideas by putting your fingerprints on them. And don't forget to inventory your family of origin. What would you like to replicate? What would you want to do differently?

3. *Take a vision retreat.* The next step in the process is processing. If you can afford to, get out of town for two days. Why? Because change of pace + change of place = change of perspective! Getting out of your routine helps you zoom out and see the big picture. Plus, new places help us think new thoughts! I'd recommend a schedule, but keep it flexible! If you're more of an intrapersonal processor, you'll need some alone time. In that case, use mealtimes to process.

4. *Write down the vision.* The goal of a vision retreat is to put something down on paper! It begins with taking inventory of your past, your passions. What makes you mad, sad, or glad? Identify the words and phrases and verses that touch a nerve ending. After you come up with a short list, compare the list with your spouse. Pay special attention to the places where those lists overlap.

5. *Rewrite the vision.* When you're coming up with the first draft of your vision or your values, use a pencil.

Remember, you're not Moses. You don't have to come down the mountain with stone tablets inscribed by the finger of God. There is an old adage: "Good writing is bad writing well edited." The same is true of vision and values. Even the Declaration of Independence was edited.

One last piece of advice: don't overshoot. If you try to identify too many values, your values lose value! If your vision is too nuanced, you probably won't even remember it. Keep it short and sweet—Jesus's vision was fifty words! And try to make it memorable!

Coat of Arms

A coat of arms is a family insignia that consists of a shield, a crest, and a motto. In medieval times, it was transmitted like a sacred trust from father to son. And while it's not an American thing, I thought it would be a fun way to celebrate my family's English heritage. So I had a coat of arms designed for the Battersons.

I had written *In a Pit with a Lion on a Snowy Day* a few years before, so we adopted the lion as our family emblem. And my life motto is "Chase the lion," so it felt like a perfect fit. Then I had the Latin version of our four values engraved on the shield. Honestly, the Latin words made it feel a little more sophisticated. And finally, I included a verse.

This is my beloved son, with whom I am well pleased.[15]

Just as the heavenly Father blessed Jesus with those words, I want to convey that same blessing to my three children. If all else fails, I want them to know they are be-loved. I also want them to know my love isn't performance-based. I love them because of who they are, not because of what they do.

It may sound like choosing our family's core values was a painless activity; however, it was anything but. We started out with a dozen potential values, then we vetted them through a process of elimination. I eventually landed on four values because there are four cardinal directions. So why not four cardinal values?

Our four family values are both *descriptive* and *prescriptive*. If I said that I always operate in a spirit of humility, I'd be lying. But when I act pridefully, I know I'm betraying the family trust. Like me, my kids fall short too. But when they do, I remind them that their failures don't define who they are! Our four values give us a frame of reference—a target to shoot at. When we miss, we realize we miss. And when we hit the bull's-eye, we try to split the arrow.

Here's the bottom line: It's impossible to lead your family if you don't know where you want to take them. It'd be like setting out on vacation with no destination in mind.

What is your vision?

What are your values?

I know some of you may be beating yourselves up at this point, feeling like you have missed the boat. And that's how I felt a decade into parenting. Every attempt at family devotions short-circuited after a few tries. I felt like I was constantly dropping the ball as a dad and a husband.

If that's you, it's time to play the man. And in my experience, your wife will appreciate the effort—any effort. So get back up, dust yourself off, and lead your family. Start creating a coat of arms and don't quit until you've provided your family with the vision and values they deserve!

The Balancing Act

One of the great challenges every man faces is juggling family and work—work-life balance. If you aren't careful, work becomes home and home becomes work. If you're going to err in putting too much effort somewhere, err on the side of family! You won't regret it.

When I speak on the subject of balance, I sometimes stand on one leg and ask the audience if I'm balanced. Some people say yes; some people say no. And they're both right and wrong. My body is constantly counterbalancing.

Such is life—all parts of it!

We all do some internal balancing as well. For example, when I was twenty-two years old, I was interviewed by a cadre of pastors called presbyters who would determine my ministerial fate. With my credentials in the balance, I expected a litany of theological questions. Instead, I was asked a single soul-piercing question: "If you had to describe yourself in one word, what would it be?" My answer? *"Driven."* At the time, I thought it was a brilliant response. Now? Not so much!

My Achilles' heel is drivenness. It's one part impatience, one part competitiveness. And neither of these things is healthy or holy. I now subscribe to long obedience in the same direction, but I still fight the unsanctified urge to do more and more in less and less time. And I'm sure I'm not alone!

If you find your identity in wealth, enough is never enough. If you find your identity in success, enough is never enough. If you find your identity in anything outside of a relationship with Christ, you'll never fill the void you feel. The only way to fill it is to find your identity in what Jesus Christ has done for you.

True freedom is having nothing to prove, and you have nothing to prove because Christ proved His love for you at the cross. That freedom allows you to play the man. You don't need to one-up anyone anymore!

One last exhortation.

The beginning of the end for King Saul was keeping a jealous eye on David. When the Israelites started celebrating David's victories more than Saul's, Saul's inferiority complex reared its ugly head. He did what weak men do—he tried to prop himself up by building monuments to himself.

Consider these two verses, separated by only one chapter:

Then Saul built an altar to the LORD.[16]

Saul went to Carmel to set up a monument to himself.[17]

When you stop building altars to God, you start building monuments to yourself. And that's the beginning of the end spiritually. You're no longer playing the man. You're playing God.

So which is it? Altars to God? Or monuments to self?

Stop playing God.

Play the man!

7

Call of Duty

*The Seventh Virtue of Manhood:
Moral Courage*

Be strong and courageous.

—Joshua 1:6

**March 30, 1981
Washington, DC**

I was in a fourth-grade gym class at Highland View Elementary School in Greendale, Wisconsin, when the principal announced over the intercom that President Ronald Reagan had been shot. Only sixty-nine days into his presidency, Reagan had just delivered a speech at the Washington Hilton. As the president exited the hotel with his entourage, John Hinckley Jr. fired a blue steel revolver six times in 1.7 seconds.[1] The first shot hit White House press secretary James Brady in the head. Another hit DC police officer Thomas Delahanty in the back of the neck. Another hit Secret Service agent Timothy McCarthy. And one .22 cartridge hit the intended target, President Reagan, lodging in his lung just one inch from his heart.

When the sound of gunshots hits the auditory cortex, one's natural reaction is to protect oneself by taking cover. And that's what everybody did, except the Secret Service agents who had been trained to react in the exact opposite fashion. Agent McCarthy instinctively did what agents do—he went into a spread eagle position, making himself the largest target possible so that he might take a bullet for the president. McCarthy is one of just four agents who have ever done so. He took a bullet to the abdomen, quite possibly saving the life of the president.

Two thousand years ago, Jesus went into a spread eagle position. He could have bailed out with one call for angelic backup, but the Creator put Himself at the mercy of His creation. Why? To make Himself the target—to take the bullet for us.

That's courage.

Courage comes in many shapes and sizes. Courage is firefighters running into a burning building when everyone else is running out. Courage is soldiers standing in the line of enemy fire. Courage is putting yourself in harm's way to protect someone else. Of course, it's one thing to do it for the president of the United States. It's an altogether different thing to do it for a run-of-the-mill sinner!

> At just the right time, when we were still powerless, Christ died for the ungodly. Very rarely will anyone die for a righteous

person, though for a good person someone might possibly dare to die. But God demonstrates his own love for us in this: While we were still sinners, Christ died for us.[2]

It took physical courage for Jesus to endure the beating and the flogging. But the most torturous part of the crucifixion wasn't the physical pain; it was feeling the wrath of God for the first time. That took unprecedented, unparalleled moral courage! He who knew no sin became sin for us! Jesus became the lightning rod of God's wrath. The theological term is *propitiation*. He absolved us from the curse by absorbing the curse Himself.

This is thin ice theologically, so let me be clear: God does not love us because Christ died for us; Christ died for us because God loves us! You mean the cross to Christ. But justice demanded that the penalty for sin be paid in full.

For thousands of years before Christ, this penalty was satisfied by an annual installment plan called the Day of Atonement. The debt was paid with animal sacrifices, but the final payment was made by the sinless Lamb of God who satisfied the righteous requirements of the law once and for all. Jesus was the final sacrifice, the final payment.

Have you ever been blamed for something that wasn't your fault? Accused of something you didn't do? It's not easy to sit there and take responsibility, is it? In fact, it's nearly impossible! Now, imagine taking the blame for everything, for everyone! That takes more than courage. It takes the highest and rarest form of courage—moral courage.

And moral courage is the seventh virtue of manhood.

"Courage is not simply one of the virtues," writes C. S. Lewis, "but the form of every virtue at the testing point."[3]

Every virtue of manhood will be tested over time, and when it is, it takes courage to pass the test. Tough love takes moral courage. So do will power and true grit. Like iron forged in fire, moral courage tempers our passion, our vision.

Wash Feet

I seldom remember my dreams, and most of the dreams I do remember have a recurrent theme—I'm late for the tip-off or kickoff of an athletic event I'm supposed to play in, and I can't seem to get there. Yes, that's my worst nightmare!

I've only had a few dreams that I would classify as God-given, but one of them was so vivid I wrote down the words I heard in my journal the moment I woke up:

> *Don't wash your hands like Pilate.*
> *Wash feet like Jesus.*

It wasn't Jesus's responsibility to wash feet. That job was reserved for the lowest servant on the Jewish totem pole. Yet Jesus took responsibility for something that wasn't His responsibility.

That's playing the man!

Pilate did the exact opposite, washing his hands as a way of saying "I'm not responsible." But washing his hands didn't absolve him of guilt. Pilate knew Jesus was innocent, yet he lacked the moral courage to let Jesus go. In the words of C. S. Lewis, "Pilate was merciful till it became risky."[4]

One verse reveals Pilate's moral weakness: "Wanting to satisfy the crowd . . . He had Jesus flogged, and handed him over to be crucified."[5]

Weak!

Simply put, Pilate was a people pleaser. He was more afraid of displeasing the crowd than he was of violating his own conscience. So he played a patsy instead of playing the man.

Are you living for the applause of people?

Or are you living for the applause of nail-scarred hands?

If you want to please God, you'll displease some people along the way. It's part and parcel of playing the man. So be it. As the old adage says, "You can please some of the people all of the time; all of the people some of the time; but you can't please all of the people all of the time."

So which is it? Wash your hands? Or wash feet?

Is there a situation where you have absolved yourself of responsibility by washing your hands instead of taking responsibility and washing someone's feet?

When we expect our wives to carry more than their fair share of the parenting responsibility, we're washing our hands instead of washing feet. When we're not pulling our weight in the workplace, we're washing our hands instead of washing feet.

So let me ask the question again: Is there a situation where you have absolved yourself of responsibility by washing your hands instead of taking responsibility and washing someone's feet?

The Sin of Silence

On April 16, 1963, Martin Luther King Jr. wrote a letter from a Birmingham jail cell challenging white clergy to step up and speak out on the issue of racial discrimination. Some clergy criticized his tactics, so King defended his strategy of nonviolent resistance.

"Injustice anywhere," warned Dr. King, "is a threat to justice everywhere."[6]

Dr. King was telling his white brothers not to wash their hands. He rebuked their do-nothingism! When we fail to use our voice, we lose our voice. And make no mistake about it, silence sanctions. Nothing says more than silence, and nothing says it louder and clearer. King accused the white church of being more cautious than courageous, remaining silent behind "the anesthetizing security of stained glass windows." And when the church cowers like that, it becomes "the archdefender of the status quo."

"We will have to repent in this generation not merely for the hateful words of bad people," warned King, "but for the appalling silence of good people."[7]

If God has spoken on a subject, how can we remain silent? To not call sin *sin* is as uncaring as not crying fire to warn others during a fire!

The sin of silence takes a wide variety of forms. Sometimes it seems as innocuous as political correctness. As I said earlier, we live in a culture where it's wrong to say something is wrong, and I think that's wrong. But we don't fight fire with fire. We should be more known for what we're for than what we're against. The best way to combat what's wrong is to do something right—write a better book, produce a better film, start a better business, draft better legislation. Criticize by creating!

With that said, we also need the moral courage to call it like we see it. To remain silent about sin is neither safe nor sound. It's the sin of tolerance. And it's cowardly. "To sin by silence," writes Ella Wheeler Wilcox, "when we should protest, makes cowards out of men."[8]

. We won't be judged only by our words. We'll also be judged by our silence—the moments when we should have spoken up.

Playing the man means speaking up when everybody else remains mute. It's saying what needs to be said. It's having the tough conversations that require tough love.

One last challenge since we're on the subject of racism.

The goal isn't being color-blind.

The goal is being color brave.[9]

We cannot—we must not—turn a blind eye to injustice. We have to step up and step in. And we can't simply point out the problem either. We must be part of the solution.

Ignoring what's wrong is moral relativism at best and cowardice at worst. Jesus told us to turn the other cheek, which takes tremendous moral courage. But He didn't tell us to turn the other way!

Modeling

Half a century ago, a psychologist named Albert Bandura did a series of studies designed to cure children who were deathly afraid of dogs. He showed the kids short videos of other children encountering dogs. The children in the videos didn't display any fear of dogs as they moved closer and closer, finally petting the dogs.

After a month of visual conditioning, the kids were placed in a similar situation to the one they had watched. An unfamiliar dog would have terrified them a month earlier, but the visual conditioning gave them newfound confidence. Most of them were able to approach the dogs and pet them.

According to Bandura's experiment, we are conditioned by what we see more than we even know. For better or for worse, we adjust our behavior to mirror the behavior of others. Bandura branded it "modeling." Forgive the pun, but fashion is a great example. We consciously and subconsciously take fashion cues, especially when we find ourselves in a new environment. We also monitor, and often mirror, everything from attitude to idiosyncrasies.

If you have young children, you witness modeling all the time. Your kids take their cues from you, and it's usually saying the same thing you wish you hadn't said. And they usually do it when you have friends over.

We involuntarily imitate the behavior of others, and we rarely even know we're doing it. For instance, sitcoms don't just entertain us, they condition us. And every movie sends a subliminal message. That's why we need to use the filter God has given us called the *conscience*. It's the key to moral courage.

Moral Compass

Remember when David cut off the corner of Saul's robe? Scripture says he was "conscience-stricken."[10] David's men wanted him to kill Saul, but David knew it was wrong. How did he know? His conscience!

The conscience is our moral compass, helping us discern right from wrong. It's our spiritual operating system—hardwired into the human heart—and it requires constant updating and upgrading. The way you do this is by downloading Scripture on a daily basis. When you study Scripture, you're uploading God's good, pleasing, and perfect will.

Then you let your conscience be your guide—a conscience informed by the Holy Scriptures and fine-tuned to the still, small voice of the Holy Spirit.

> Start children off on the way they should go; and even when they are old they will not turn from it.[11]

That's my goal as a parent, and the key to achieving that goal is conscience. It's the inner-parent when a parent isn't present. Ultimately, I want my kids to do the right thing when I'm not there. I want them to live according to their consciences, their convictions.

If you violate your conscience consistently, it's like a gauge that no longer gauges. But if you get into God's Word and God's presence on a consistent basis, your conscience learns to listen for and respond to the voice of the Holy Spirit. Eventually you become a man after God's own heart like King David himself.

Playing the man is letting your conscience be your guide.

That's what Dr. Martin Luther King Jr. did.

That's what Martin Luther did hundreds of years before him.

Both men were as imperfect as you and me, but they had moral courage in rare quantity. King spoke up against racial discrimination, while Luther stood up against the selling of indulgences. Each one attempted to right a wrong via moral courage.

On November 31, 1517, Martin Luther transcribed and translated his conscience concerning the question of indulgences into his *Ninety-five Theses*, posting them on the doors of the Castle Church. When told to recant at the Diet of

Worms, Luther said, "My conscience is captive to the Word of God. I cannot and I will not recant anything, for to go against conscience is neither right nor safe."[12] This began the Protestant Reformation.

Where does moral courage come from? From a conscience that is taken captive by the Word of God. Moral courage isn't swayed by public opinion or a Supreme Court decision. Our plumb line is Scripture, plain and simple!

A man of conscience is a change agent—a force to be reckoned with. As Andrew Jackson observed, "One man with courage makes a majority."[13] He's not blown here and there by trending winds. He's anchored to the Word of God, and that anchor holds him through ups and downs, through thick and thin.

Conformity

On August 10, 1948, a pioneering television producer named Allen Funt debuted a hidden-camera reality TV show called *Candid Camera*. The genius of the show is that it caught people in the act of being themselves. It produced lots of laughs, but it also offered a fascinating look into the human psyche.

In one episode titled "Face the Rear," an unsuspecting person boarded an elevator and naturally turned around to face the front of the elevator. That's when three actors entered the elevator and faced the rear. Hidden cameras in the elevator captured the angst of the prankee. To turn or not to turn? Finally, a fourth actor entered the elevator and faced the rear. Without exception, the person facing the front would turn around and face the rear. The social influence exerted by those facing the rear was too overwhelming for that person to remain the only one facing the front.

Now, juxtapose that with this:

> Do not conform to the pattern of this world, but be transformed by the renewing of your mind.[14]

The NLT says, "Don't copy the behavior and customs of this world." That's easier said than done, isn't it? Especially when dominant culture is facing the rear.

Simply put, conformity is cowardice. It's taking the path of least or no resistance. You can play the game according to the rules established by dominant culture. But even if you win, you lose!

Where have you conformed to culture? Think about it—because that is precisely where you need to be transformed.

The Courage of Confession

Moral courage starts with confession, and Martin Luther makes a good case study. Before visiting the Castle Church in Wittenberg, Germany, several years ago, I decided to read a Luther biography. Luther had his blind spots, like the rest of us. But the most striking thing I discovered was that he would sometimes spend up to six hours confessing sin in a single sitting. Either Luther had an oversensitive conscience or he understood the power of confession. I'm guessing it was the latter, not the former.

Here's the reality: most of us haven't spent more than six minutes confessing sin. In fact, we usually take about six seconds: *Lord, forgive me for everything I've ever done wrong. Amen.* The problem with that is this: vague confessions result in a vague feeling of forgiveness.

If you really want to be courageous, try writing your confession. I'd encourage you to destroy that piece of paper after you're done confessing, but it might help you identify the specific thoughts, behaviors, and attitudes you're trying to change.

If you want to exercise even more courage than that, confess your sin to a trusted confidant. It's often more difficult confessing to another person than it is to God, and that's why it's good for us. It also invites that person into your problem. Who knows, maybe they're part of the solution.

Over the years, I've heard quite a few confessions from men who struggle with lust, pride, greed, and anger—just like I do. And I've heard a few confessions that would make your head swivel. But I can honestly say that my respect for the person confessing has never gone down, regardless of what they've confessed. In fact, my respect for them goes up. Why? Because it takes moral courage to confess your sins. And that kind of courage breaks the enemy's stranglehold on our lives.

Is there a confession you need to make to your wife, to a friend?

Or maybe you need counseling to help you overcome an addiction?

Play the man!

And don't just confess your sin. Confess your weaknesses. Confess your fears. Confess your hurts. This isn't easy to do, but putting on a brave face isn't always brave. It's often cowardly! True courage is being vulnerable enough to admit your faults and foibles.

You cannot experience intimacy without vulnerability. You don't need to *over*share! And I'm not talking about TMI—too much information. But you do need to open your heart and your ears. Sometimes our male utilitarianism is a wonderful quality—*get 'er done!* But your wife doesn't always want you to try to solve the problem. Sometimes she just wants a little empathy, a little vulnerability.

Bold Humility

Courage starts with confession, but it doesn't stop there. The next step is profession, which is often as difficult for men as confession is. Sure, some athletes give God a little shout-out after scoring a touchdown or hitting a game-winning three-pointer. And that's great. But playing the man means more than that. It's being unashamed of the gospel because it's the power of God unto salvation![15] I'm not talking about in-your-face evangelism or Bible thumping. That often does more harm than good if it's done in the wrong spirit. Playing the man means being a bold witness for Jesus Christ, but doing so in a spirit of humility.

It's bold humility or humble boldness, take your pick.

A few months after denying Christ, Peter was standing before the same Sanhedrin that scared him into his infamous denial. But something was different this time. The religious leaders were trying to shut Peter down, but Peter wouldn't shut up.

> When they saw the courage of Peter and John and realized that they were unschooled, ordinary men, they were astonished and they took note that they had been with Jesus.[16]

Peter wasn't afraid anymore. Why? Because he witnessed the resurrection of Jesus Christ. How could you be afraid of anything after that? Plus, Peter had been filled with the Holy Spirit.

> For the Spirit God gave us does not make us timid, but gives us power, love and self-discipline.[17]

The Holy Spirit gives us the moral courage to confess our sin and profess our faith. He gives us the courage to attempt things we cannot do in our own strength. He gives us the courage to play the man no matter what, no matter when, no matter where!

The word *proselytize* has become a dirty word in our culture, but nothing is more gracious or generous than sharing your faith with someone—you are sharing what is most important and sacred to you. I think of it this way: worship is *bragging about God to God* and evangelism is *bragging about God to others*. So evangelism is one more way of worshiping God.

Penn Jillette is one half of Penn & Teller, an ongoing comedy and magic act that headlines a show in Las Vegas. Penn is a self-proclaimed atheist, but he's an atheist who has no respect for those who don't proselytize! After one of his shows, a middle-aged man politely and respectfully gave him a Gideon Bible. Penn doesn't believe a word the Bible has to say, but he respected the gesture. Why? Because that man believed enough to proselytize!

"If you believe in heaven and hell," says Penn, "how much do you have to hate someone to *not* proselytize?" Good question! Then Penn says point-blank, "I don't respect people who don't proselytize!"[18]

Do we believe what we believe enough to help others believe? Or do we not? The greatest gift you can give someone is your faith. So play the man by professing your faith!

Crash Helmets

In his book *The Barbarian Way*, Erwin McManus makes the fun observation that a group of buzzards is called a "committee." How apropos! He also observes that a group of rhinos is called a "crash." A rhino can run thirty miles per hour, which is pretty impressive considering the fact that they can weigh up to five thousand pounds!

A group of men without a mission is a committee, and they usually act like buzzards. But a group of men with moral courage is a crash, and the gates of hell will not prevail against that kind of battering ram.

Faithfulness is not holding the fort.

It's taking back enemy territory!

Two thousand years ago, Jesus gave us a green light. He said, "Go and make disciples of all nations."[19]

It's not ready, set, go.

It's go, set, ready!

"On the whole, I do not find Christians, outside the catacombs, sufficiently sensible of conditions," notes author Annie Dillard. "Does anyone have the foggiest idea what sort of power we so blithely invoke? Or as I suspect, does no one believe a word of it?" That's a stinging rebuke, but it's hard to argue with it when you look at the average Christian or the average church. Then Annie playfully yet powerfully prods, "It is madness to wear ladies' straw hats and velvet hats to church; we should all be wearing crash helmets."[20]

Play the Man is more than a book; it's a wake-up call. Like smelling salts, we need the Spirit of God to activate our sympathetic nervous system. We must awaken to realize what's at stake. We were born on a battlefield between good and evil, and we must choose sides. Then we must fight the good fight.

I have a friend, Mike Foster, who cofounded www.xxx church.com in 2002. Mike has a heart for men who struggle with porn addiction, but he also has a heart for the porn industry. That's why he set up a booth at a porn convention and handed out *Jesus Loves Porn Stars* Bibles. That takes courage, the kind of courage Peter embodied when he stood up to the religious establishment.

Permission to speak frankly?

We can pray "Your kingdom come, Your will be done" until we're blue in the face, but it won't make any difference if we hunker down in the comfortable confines of our Christian subculture. We need to invade some hellholes with the light and love of Jesus Christ.

"Some want to live within the sound of church or chapel bell," said missionary C. T. Studd. "I want to run a rescue shop within a yard of hell." The church needs more Studds! And you can quote me on that.[21]

Jesus didn't die to keep us safe.

Jesus died to make us dangerous.

Play Offense

"I will build my church, and the gates of Hades will not overcome it."[22]

Translation: *we win!* But you wouldn't know it by the way some people fret and fuss. Come on, men. Come on, church.

There is no place for a defeatist attitude in the kingdom of God. His kingdom will come—it's unstoppable, it's inevitable! Jesus didn't say *you* will build *your* church. If He had, that would be cause for concern. Jesus said *I* will build *My* church—emphasis on *I* and *My*.

By definition, gates are defensive measures. So the church is called to play offense! The enemy wants to get you on your heels, put you on the defensive. But playing the man is playing offense with your life, with your marriage, with your faith.

I've pastored a church in the epicenter of politics for two decades now, and I've observed that the level of angst goes way up during election years. In one sense that's normal and natural. For the people who live in the nation's capital, jobs are on the line every election cycle. But why do we get so nervous about who will win the White House, who will control Congress, or who will get appointed to the Supreme Court? Don't get me wrong. I still believe God wants to raise up Josephs, Daniels, and Nehemiahs. But just in case you've forgotten, we already have a King! His name is "Wonderful Counselor, Mighty God, Everlasting Father, Prince of Peace. Of the increase of his government and peace there will be no end."[23]

Do I want God-fearing, Bible-believing people in political office? Absolutely! But the anchor of my hope isn't a president, a senator, or a Supreme Court justice. God is still on His throne. And while we may not know what the future holds, we know who holds the future!

I recently had dinner with the pastor of All Saints Church in Worchester, England. I shared a little bit of our history at National Community Church, which dates back to 1996. To be honest, that feels like forever to me. Then he shared the history of All Saints Church, and it put my history into perspective. Their church building dates all the way back to AD 680, and their current Anglo-Saxon church was built on top of a Roman church that was named after Emperor Constantine's mother, Helena.

It's been continuously worshiped in for more than thirteen hundred years!

That pastor has a much longer view than I do, and I think that makes him less nervous. Kings and queens come and go, just like presidents. In fact, empires rise and fall. But God's kingdom has been coming for two thousand years, and it cannot be stopped. It's an invisible kingdom, an eternal kingdom. The kingdom of God has survived every threat against it. And it has not just survived—it has thrived. It's advancing faster than ever before. By the most conservative estimates, a hundred thousand people around the globe put their faith in Jesus Christ every single day. That's more people than there are seconds in a day, which means there is rejoicing in heaven every single second of every single day!

Take heart.

Take courage.

Play the man!

PART 2

MAKE THE MAN

THE RITE OF PASSAGE

8

No Man's Land

He shall turn the heart of the fathers to the children, and the heart of the children to their fathers.

—Malachi 4:6 KJV

August 1898
Flag Springs, Texas

Sam Rayburn served as speaker of the house for seventeen years, the longest tenure in US history. And he was arguably the most powerful person in Washington during that tenure. No bill came to a vote without his consent, and he could orchestrate a filibuster with the best of them. Sam served twenty-four terms as a member of Congress, but he never lost touch with his roots.

Sam grew up on a forty-acre cotton farm with his ten siblings in Flag Springs, Texas. At eighteen, Sam headed off to East Texas Normal College. His family was dirt poor.

Sam didn't even have a suitcase, so he bundled his clothes and tied them with a rope. Few words were exchanged between father and son on the way to the train station. Then, when the train pulled into the station and Sam was about to board, his father reached into his pocket and pulled out a fistful of money.

"Only God knows how he saved it," said Sam. "He never had any extra money. We earned just enough to live. It broke me up, him handing me that twenty-five dollars. I often wondered what he did without, what sacrifice he and my mother made."[1]

Just before a teary-eyed Sam boarded the train, his father grasped his hands and spoke four words that would echo in Sam's ear forever: "Sam, be a man!"[2]

Looking back on the landscape of his seventy-eight years, Sam Rayburn identified that exchange with his father as a monumental moment. It was a reference point for the rest of his life. And that's our job as fathers—to give our sons a reference point.

I share that story for two reasons.

First, our most sacred responsibility as fathers is to help our sons play the man. Commission your son with a Discipleship Covenant and give him a Rite of Passage. Otherwise, we exile them to *no man's land*.

So the question is this: How do you make a man? And that's what we'll explore in the last three chapters of this book.

The Discipleship Covenant I detail in the next chapter and the Rite of Passage I describe in the final chapter were my way of saying to my sons—be a man! My goal was to give them a reference point for manhood.

The second reason I share this story is to remind you that one act of intentionality can change the trajectory of your son's life. So be encouraged, because a little effort goes a long way. Your words will echo in their ears forever. Your deeds will make a difference long after you are gone.

Last Will and Testament

In 480 BC, King Xerxes and his million-man Persian army invaded Greece and demanded Sparta surrender their arms.[3] No one would have blamed King Leonidas for surrendering. After all, his battalion was outnumbered a thousand to one. But Leonidas decided that it was better to die courageously than to live cowardly. So he uttered his famous last words, "Come and take them!"[4]

For three days, three hundred Spartans held the narrow pass at Thermopylae in one of history's most famous last stands. They selflessly sacrificed themselves so the rest of the army could retreat to safety. The Greek historian Herodotus described their last stand this way: "Here they defended themselves to the last, those who still had swords using them, and the others resisting with their hands and teeth."[5]

Last words carry unusual weight.

Last words are symbolic and prophetic.

This was true of King Leonidas—his last words were fighting words! And it was true of Malachi, the prophet who got the last word in the Old Testament. The very last verse of the Old Testament is like a last will and testament.

He shall turn the heart of the fathers to their children, and the heart of the children to their fathers, lest I come and smite the land with a curse.[6]

157

These are more than the last words of the Old Testament. I believe these words compose the last prayer, the last hope. It's the turnkey to revival in our nation, but it starts in the family—with fathers. God wants to turn the heart of the fathers to their children, but it can't be a half turn. Not if we want a turnaround.

Let me shoot straight.

I'm praying for a spiritual awakening in America—we need nothing less, nothing else. And I'd love for it to start in the city where I pastor, Washington, DC. But the reality is this: revival always starts in the heart, in the home. Then, and only then, does it spread to cities and nations.

To some it may sound like a minor note—turning the heart of the fathers to their children. But it's a major chord. It's the way we break generational curses and pass on generational blessings. And Malachi singled out fathers for a reason.

I love mothers. I honor mothers. And parenting is a tag-team sport. But if mothers aren't the primary problem, then they aren't the ultimate solution. The problem and the solution lie with fathers. There are exceptions to this rule, but mothers generally bond more naturally with their children. One reason is the obvious fact that they gave birth to them!

It's men who have dropped the ball, dropped the baton.

Pass the Baton

When I was in junior high, I was part of a 4×100-meter relay—Batterson, Elko, Simchak, Julian. All four of us were fast, so fast that our record still stands three decades later. How do I know this? Because every time I'm in Naperville,

Illinois, I revisit Madison Junior High to make sure. Yet despite our record-setting time, we didn't win the city championship. Why? Because I dropped the baton as it was handed to me. It ranks as one of my most painful athletic memories.

In a similar fashion, too many dads are dropping the baton of faith.

We don't give our children a running start because we don't know how to hand off our faith—what we know about life, love, and the Lord. I know it's difficult to do for your son what your dad may not have done for you, but it's no excuse. You must hand the baton to your son, then run behind him and cheer him on for as long you can keep up.

How does it start? In the heart!

It's hard for me to pinpoint one moment when my heart shifted, but the genesis was a tough conversation with my wife, Lora. We were on vacation when Lora said something that I didn't see coming: "This isn't what I signed up for." That'll get your attention in a hurry! Especially when your wife is loving and patient like mine.

At the time, I was pastoring a growing church, writing a book or two per year, and traveling to speak at conferences about thirty days a year. Remember my Achilles' heel—*drivenness*? It was getting the best of me, and my family was getting the rest of me, which wasn't much!

Something shifted in my heart that day, and I made some difficult decisions. First, I put some boundary stones back in place. I limited myself to twelve overnight speaking trips per year. Have we had some bumps in the road? Of course! Maintaining the right rhythm of family life and work life is a constant challenge. But looking back, that one decision probably saved my family—and my sanity.

Also, right around that time, I read a book by Andy Stanley titled *Choosing to Cheat*. One statement I read in the book totally changed my perspective: "To say *yes* to one thing is to say *no* to the other."[7] I decided to say no to a lot more opportunities so I could say yes to my top priorities—my wife and children.

At the end of the day, I want to be famous in my home. But it's hard to be famous in your home if you're never home!

I also put a few other boundaries in place.

I started guarding my Sabbath religiously. In my case, Sabbath is Monday. So every Monday, Lora and I have a coffee date. Sometimes we talk about budget and calendar. More often than not we talk about our kids. Those coffee dates set the tone for the entire week.

I also instituted something I call an FSM with my oldest son, Parker. The acronym stands for Father-Son Meeting, and we met on Tuesday nights during his Year of Discipleship. I look back on it with some mixed emotions because I think I could have done a better job being more intentional, but I also didn't want it to come across as an assignment or a class-like commitment. So we'd hit a coffeehouse or a Barnes and Noble or a favorite restaurant and talk about the week, the books we were reading together, or life in general.

If you want your heart to turn toward your children, you have to spend time with them—quality time and quantity time. There are no shortcuts.

Family First

One of my all-time favorite authors is Aiden Wilson Tozer. His books have had an unparalleled impact on my spiritual journey. But truth be told, I was disappointed when I read his biography. This doesn't discredit everything he did as a pastor and a writer, but I think Tozer failed the most important test. When he died, his wife, Ada, remarried. Several years into her second marriage, a friend asked Ada to describe the difference between her first husband and second husband, her first marriage and second marriage.

"I have never been happier in my life," said Ada. "Aiden loved Jesus Christ, but Leonard Odam loves me."[8]

Let's strive for both—loving Jesus and loving our wives!

One of my mantras is "family first." In reality, it's God first, but that's assumed. Here's what I mean by family first: if a conflict arises between family and anything else, family comes first.

When Parker was in elementary school, I coached his basketball team. Most of those games were on Saturday nights, creating a schedule conflict with our church's two Saturday night services. I made the difficult decision to cancel one of our Saturday night services because coaching my son was a priority, and I didn't make up a fake excuse. I simply explained to our congregation why we were canceling the second service. Was it misunderstood by a few people? I'm sure it was. But it modeled *family first* to our church and, more important, to our kids.

One of my longstanding rules is answering the phone if my wife or kids call. It doesn't matter what I'm doing or who I'm with. *Sorry, Mr. President, my daughter is calling.* I want my family to know they are more important to me than whomever it is that I'm meeting with. And I make no apologies. I've even answered my phone in the middle of a sermon a time or two. Now, sometimes I'll text my wife or kids and ask if it's urgent. But availability is a high value for me. It's a small way I can show them what a big deal they are to me.

What boundaries do you need to put in place to protect yourself?

To protect your marriage?

To protect your family?

Implementing such boundaries requires making difficult decisions, but they'll probably be the best ones you ever make. You won't regret prioritizing your family. And that decision will echo in the lives of your children forever.

I know our families can become idols in our lives. And I know some parents who live vicariously through their children to such a degree that their emotional well-being is tied to their children's performance. That's not healthy or holy. But neither is negligence.

If I had to describe my dad in a single phrase, it would be this: he was there for me. And that is high praise! He may not have taken me through the kind of proactive plan I'm prescribing, but he was incredibly loving and wise.

As a kid, my life was sports. And I don't think my dad missed a single game growing up—baseball, basketball, or football. He made it to most of the practices too.

While attending the University of Chicago, where I played basketball, our team traveled all across the country, and my dad drove ridiculous distances to watch me play. The most memorable was a game at Brandeis University in Boston, Massachusetts. My mom and dad drove all the way from Chicago to watch me play five minutes in the second half of that game. Yes, I was a little ticked at my coach. The amazing thing is that my parents had to turn around and drive home the same night. A thirty-hour road trip to watch me play for five minutes.

That's something you never forget. And I think that's half the battle—being there for your kids. But to be truly successful, you also need a battle plan.

Pray the Man

The *Queen Mary* is one of the largest and most famous cruise ships in the world. It's now retired and permanently moored in Long Beach, California. During her sailing days, she made 1,001 transatlantic crossings. *Queen Mary* is 181 feet tall and 1,019 feet long. She weighs 81,237 tons, including a 45-ton anchor.[9] But like any ship of any size, she is guided by a rather small rudder. And on that rudder is a tiny device called the trim tab. The trim tab turns the ship.

Prayer is the trim tab that turns the heart.

You can't play the man if you don't pray the price. That's how God turns the heart. You'll never be a perfect parent, but you can be a praying parent. And prayer is what turns ordinary parents into prophets who shape the destiny of their children.

Over the years, I've tried every parenting methodology on the market. I've dared to discipline, raised modern-day knights, and grown kids God's way. And while those methodologies contain some great ideologies, following them hasn't always resulted in a new kid by Friday!

After two decades of parenting, I have less confidence in me and my methodologies. But I have more confidence in a heavenly Father who hears and answers prayer. That is where parenting starts—with prayer.

I've written an entire book on the topic of parenting titled *Praying Circles around the Lives of Your Children.* So I won't dive deep into this subject. But let me share, once again, the prayer I've prayed thousands of times. It's my go-to prayer, a touchstone prayer that my children will remember the rest of their lives. It's my adaptation of Luke 2:52—*May you grow in wisdom and stature and in favor with God and with man.*

I've seen God answer this prayer in so many ways over the years. And I can't wait to see how He continues to answer it. But one word of caution seems wise right here.

Prayer is like a boomerang. It sometimes seems like the answer is getting farther and farther away, especially during the teenage years. Don't get discouraged. Keep claiming God's promises for your kids. Sooner or later, the answer to your prayer will come out of nowhere, often when you least expect it.

Pray the man.

The First Word

If I were to give one hundred pastors a pop quiz and ask them to identify the focal point of John the Baptist's ministry, I'm guessing ninety-nine would simply say: to prepare the way for the Lord. And they wouldn't be wrong, but they wouldn't be entirely right either. The primary objective of John's ministry was prophesied about him before his birth. An angel said to his father, Zechariah,

> He will be great in the sight of the Lord. He is never to take wine or other fermented drink, and he will be filled with the Holy Spirit even before he is born. He will bring back many of the people of Israel to the Lord their God. And he will go on before the Lord, in the spirit and power of Elijah, to turn the hearts of the parents to their children.[10]

That last statement echoes the last verse of Malachi, and it must have jogged Zechariah's memory of Malachi 4:6. That last prayer in the Old Testament is the opening promise in the New Testament. Coincidence? I think not. This was the mission, the vision that John the Baptist was willing to die for.

I once spent an unforgettable day in Paris with my wife and daughter. After visiting the Eiffel Tower and Arc de Triomphe, we had one hour to tour the Louvre. We made a beeline for the most famous portrait, the *Mona Lisa*. But along the way I noticed a rather grotesque piece of art—a man's head on a platter. You guessed it—it was John the Baptist. It wasn't beautiful. But it was. But it wasn't. But it was.

Here's the backstory.

John the Baptist was a man's man—you automatically qualify for that club if you eat locusts and wear camel hair. But it was moral courage that set John apart. When Herod married his brother's wife, Herodias, John the Baptist wouldn't sanction the marriage, so Herod had John thrown in jail. Then during a crazy dance party, an intoxicated Herod offered Herodias's daughter anything she wanted. Prompted by her evil mother, she asked for John's head on a platter.

We don't know what went through John's mind as he was about to be beheaded, but I don't think he second-guessed anything he had said or done. In fact, I think he would have played his cards the same way all over again. Why? Because John wasn't playing games, he was playing the man.

As I stood in the Louvre and looked at this gruesome yet handsome piece of art, I couldn't help but wonder if modernity has ignored what medievals celebrated. A head on a platter is grotesque, no doubt. But is anything more noble, more powerful, than a man who plays the man—a man who is willing to live and die for what he believes in?

The last chapter of John the Baptist's life reminds me of Scotland's hero, William Wallace. In the 1995 movie *Braveheart*, before going to the gallows, Wallace utters some powerful last words and the Scottish accent makes them sound even more epic! Wallace says, "Every man dies. Not every man really lives."[11]

So true!

Play the man!

Make the man!

9

The Discipleship Covenant

This is my beloved Son, with whom I am well
pleased.

—Matthew 3:17 ESV

September 2, 2013
Havana, Cuba

When Diana Nyad was nine years old, she stood on a beach in
Fort Lauderdale, Florida. A hundred nautical miles away, Fidel
Castro's revolution was in full swing. "Where is Cuba, Mom?"
asked Diana. "I can't see it. Exactly where is it out there?"

Diana's mother pulled her close as they gazed at the seem-
ingly endless ocean. Then she pointed toward the horizon.
"There," she said. "It's right over there. You can't see it but
it's so close you could almost swim there."[1]

That day a dream was conceived in Diana's heart—a
dream of becoming the first person to swim across the straits
of Florida. When Diana tried and failed in 1978 at the age of

twenty-nine, the dream went dormant for more than three decades, but it did not die. In 2011, Diana tried and failed again. And again. And again.

Then, on September 2, 2013, an indefatigable Diana gave it one more try at sixty-four years of age. Her motto? "Find a way." And that's what she did. She found her way through ocean waters infested with aggressive whitetip sharks and venomous box jellyfish. She found her way through inky black waters, dehydration, and hallucinations. Fifty-three hours and 110 statute miles later, Diana Nyad fulfilled her dream and became the first person to swim from Cuba to Florida without the help of a shark cage.

"I have three messages," said Diana, her words slurred by a swollen tongue. "One is we should never, ever give up. Two is you never are too old to chase your dreams. Three is it looks like a solitary sport, but it's a team."[2]

How did Diana do what no one had done before? What enabled her to endure that kind of physical and mental punishment? And why?

In her words, "You must set your will."[3] It's the third virtue—will power. It also took raw passion, clear vision, and true grit. But Diana didn't accomplish the dream all by herself; it took a team of people. Diana's dream team was thirty-five strong. And there was a cardinal rule among the team members during Diana's swim: nobody reveals to her where she is or how far she has to go!

The mind-set, the team, the rules—all of them were keys to accomplishing what had never been done before. But there was one more factor—her father. When Diana turned five, her Greek-Egyptian father, Aristotle Nyad, excitedly called her into his den and unveiled her destiny.

"I have been waiting so very long for zis day," said Aristotle in his thick Greek accent. "Now you arre five. Today iz the day you are rready to understand ze most significant zing I will ever tell you, darrling." Aristotle opened an unabridged dictionary on his desk and pointed to her name. "Let me tell you somezing, darrling. Tomorrow you will go to your little preschool and you will ask your little friends iz hiz name in ze dictionary? Zey will tell you no. You arre ze only one, darrling. You arre ze special one."[4]

Then Aristotle pulled back the curtain, revealing the meaning of her name: "Yourr name: Nyad {naiad}. Firrst definition, from Grreek mythology, the nymphs zat swam in the lakes, oceans, rrivers, and fountains to prrotect ze waters forr ze gods. Listen to me, darrling, because now iz coming ze most important part. Next, says, a girrl or woman champion swimmer. Darrling, zis is yourr destiny!"[5]

God has given you naming rights as a father. It's an awesome privilege and responsibility. Naming rights begin at birth, but they don't end there. You name your child and nickname them their entire lives. It's your job to name their gifts, name their passions, and name their character. Then you call out their God-given potential through tough love, patient discipline, and endless encouragement.

The power of life and death is in the tongue.[6] And that's doubly true of fathers—your words carry unusual weight. You have the power to bless or to curse! Your words give your children something to live up to or something to live down to.

You are more than a father.

You are a priest, a prophet to your children.

No one knows your child better than you do. In some ways, you know them better than they know themselves because you remember them before they started remembering. So you are a historian, a biographer. But you are also an oracle. Like Diana's father, it's your responsibility to help your children discover their destiny. Then you get behind them and help them go for it.

It's a father's job to recognize teachable moments.

It's a father's job to create teachable moments.

That's where a Discipleship Covenant comes into play.

The Discipleship Covenant

As my oldest son, Parker, approached his twelfth birthday, I spent months prayerfully crafting a Discipleship Covenant. You'll probably be underwhelmed when you read it. Honestly, there is nothing groundbreaking or earth-shattering about it. But it was a game changer because it gave me a game plan for his Year of Discipleship.

It was my way of making a man out of him.

When it came time to present the covenant to Parker, I wanted to do it someplace special, someplace memorable. He loves to camp, so we drove an hour south of DC to Pohick Bay on the Potomac River. We set up camp, cooked hot dogs over the fire, and did some stargazing. Then, after tucking his younger brother, Josiah, into his sleeping bag, I pulled out the Discipleship Covenant I had created.

For the record, an angelic choir did not appear in the sky singing the "Hallelujah Chorus"! Honestly, it felt like an ordinary camping trip until that moment. In the glow of the campfire, I explained the three challenges—physical, mental, and spiritual. Then we cut ourselves and signed the covenant in blood. All right, that's not true. We used regular ink, but it was a poignant moment nonetheless.

Before unpacking the three challenges, here's a copy of the Discipleship Covenant I signed with Josiah a few years later. It's very similar to the one Parker and I signed, with a few tweaks. I made a few edits because my sons are very different. And I'd encourage you to do the same. Don't just adopt it; adapt it.

THE
Son's Covenant

I, Josiah, promise to commit myself to a year of discipleship with my dad.

I will submit to my dad's leadership and instruction with humility, respect, and a teachable spirit. I recognize that part of discipleship is discipline. I also pledge myself to complete three challenges—a physical challenge, intellectual challenge, and spiritual challenge.

THE PHYSICAL CHALLENGE

"Do you not know that your bodies are temples of the Holy Spirit, who is in you, whom you have received from God? You are not your own; you were bought at a price. Therefore honor God with your bodies."

1 Corinthians 6:19–20

I will seek to honor God with my body because my body is a temple of the Holy Spirit. I will discipline myself and stretch myself so that I can say like Paul—I have finished the race.

I, Josiah, will train for a century bike ride with my dad.

171

The Intellectual Challenge

"Love the Lord your God with all your heart and with all your soul and with all your mind."

Matthew 22:37

I will stretch my mind by learning new things. I will cultivate a teachable spirit in all things at all times. I will also keep a journal to keep track of the lessons God is teaching me.

I, Josiah, pledge to read twelve books and discuss them with my dad.

The Spiritual Challenge

"Don't let anyone look down on you because you are young, but set an example for the believers in speech, in conduct, in love, in faith and in purity."

1 Timothy 4:12

This is a year to ask questions and seek God. I will follow in the footsteps of Jesus by serving others. I will seek to discover my spiritual gifts and fan them into flame.

I, Josiah, pledge to read the entire New Testament this year.

As part of my spiritual training, I will complete a forty-day media fast during Lent. I will also seek to live according to our four family values and establish a list of life goals.

I, Josiah, make this solemn oath on February 16, 2014.

_____

SIGNATURE

THE
Father's Covenant

I, Mark, do solemnly swear to disciple my son to the best of my God-given ability over the next year. I will fast with my son and pray for my son. I will share my experience and wisdom with kindness and encouragement. And I will do my best to help Josiah meet the physical, spiritual, and intellectual challenges he will face this year.

I promise to make time each week for a Father-Son Meeting. We will talk about God and talk about life. Every question is a good question. And I will do my best to answer every question honestly and openly.

I will seek to model the lessons I want my son to learn. I will admit when I'm wrong and ask for forgiveness. And I will seek to bless my son with the same blessing bestowed upon Jesus by His heavenly Father:

> *"This is my beloved Son, in whom I am well pleased."*
> *Matthew 3:17 KJV*

I will seek to help Josiah discover the gifts, passions, and convictions that will guide his life. I will seek to help my son find his true identity in Christ. And I will seek to help Josiah discover a sense of destiny that is his birthright as a child of God and by virtue of his namesake, King Josiah.

> *"[King Josiah] did that which was right in the sight of the LORD, and walked in all the way of David his father, and turned not aside to the right hand or to the left."*
> *2 Kings 22:2 KJV*

> I hereby pledge that, upon Josiah's completion of the physical, spiritual, and intellectual challenges set forth in this covenant, I will take my son on a pilgrimage to a place of mutual choice. This pilgrimage will be a celebration of his accomplishments during this year and a Rite of Passage into his teenage years.
>
> _____
>
> SIGNATURE

When, Where, How

As you craft your covenant, remember that you are writing for a preteen or teen. You don't have to speak King James English! And it doesn't have to be on par with the Declaration of Independence or the Gettysburg Address. The words don't matter as much as the spirit behind them. The covenant itself sends a powerful message to your son. It conveys your commitment as a father—a commitment to give him everything you've got as a father.

Now, let me answer a few frequently asked questions.

When should I initiate the Year of Discipleship?

There is an old axiom: "When the student is ready, the teacher appears."

You know your son better than anyone, and you'll know when he is ready. I chose my sons' twelfth birthdays because I wanted their rites of passage to coincide with their thirteenth birthdays—the year they became teenagers.

There is no "magic age," because kids mature at different times and in different ways. Preteens are like wet cement, which makes the process a little easier. Plus, dads are still cool at that age! Of course, if you wait until they are a little older, you can upgrade the quality of conversations because they're dealing with teen issues. In my opinion, the ideal window is between twelve and sixteen years old. But remember, children are never too old to be discipled!

Where should I do the covenant signing?

The simplest answer is someplace special, someplace memorable. Is there a place you know your son loves? The mountains? The ocean? I took Parker camping in a tent, but with Josiah I rented a cabin. One way or the other, I recommend a change of scenery. Remember this little formula, which I mentioned in chapter 6: change of pace + change of place = change of perspective.

For the record, I recommend one-on-one—just father and son. But if you have older sons or uncles or even a grandfather you want to include, have at it. Surrounding your son with a circle of elders will enhance the entire Year of Discipleship.

Does it have to be a retreat?

I highly recommend an overnight. That's critical. And start with a nice dinner. When you're at the table, set the tone for the next twenty-four hours. Share your heart for your son by sharing stories. Begin by affirming who he is. Then reaffirm your commitment to him as his father. This is a solemn event, but remember to have some fun too! Keep the focus on the covenant, but couch it in good memories of a good time. In fact, if you can add an element of adventure, all the better. Why not hike to the top of a mountain and present the covenant there.

With Josiah, I presented the Discipleship Covenant after we got settled in at the cabin. I let him read the covenant, and then I unpacked it. After talking about the three challenges, we knelt and prayed, consecrating ourselves to God and to each other. Then Josiah signed the covenant while I covertly captured a photo.

How collaborative should the process be?

If you want your son to take ownership of the Discipleship Covenant, you had better make sure he's in lockstep with the challenges. As a student of your children, you should have a good idea of the physical challenge that will fit his physique. You'll also know the kinds of books he likes to read. That's a good starting point. But one of the best ways to get him to take full ownership is to stop, collaborate, and listen. Let your son recommend some books he wants to read or figure out what kind of fast he wants to do during Lent. And when the covenant is complete, make sure your son has 100 percent buy in on the Rite of Passage pilgrimage. Do this by giving him a few options, then letting him choose where you go and what you do.

Did you do something similar with your daughter?

I didn't do a Discipleship Covenant with Summer, and I sometimes second-guess that decision. For better or for worse, I felt like Lora needed to take the reins and be more hands-on with Summer, which she did.

That said, a father's relationship with his daughter is important beyond words. While I didn't do a Year of Discipleship with her, I did do a Rite of Passage. As I described in chapter 4, we trained for the Escape from Alcatraz swim for several months, and then we flew out to San Francisco for a special weekend. The highlight for me was taking her to a beautiful restaurant overlooking the Pacific Ocean. That's when I gave her a heart-shaped necklace and told her that her heart belonged to me until she gave her heart to the man she would marry.

Lora also did a Rite of Passage with Summer and her aunts that I detail in *Praying Circles around the Lives of Your Children*. They took the train up to New York City, saw a Broadway play, and presented her with a poster with nine words—words that define who she is, who she is becoming!

Now, let me break down the three challenges.

The Physical Challenge

As a kid, my world was sports. I ate, drank, and breathed baseball, basketball, and football, but that isn't where either of my sons' interests lie. But no matter how your son is wired, a physical challenge is significant. Why? Because your body is a temple of the Holy Spirit, and it must be stewarded. Plus, physical disciplines and spiritual disciplines are not unrelated. It's a package deal.

You must be a student of your son. You want to push him past his comfort zone, but you must do it in a way that is motivating. Push him hard enough to prove to him that he is capable of more than he thought he was. With Parker, I was tempted to do a 10K run. That would have pushed me, but Parker is a jackrabbit, so I didn't feel like that would prove

Mark and Parker celebrate crossing the finish line.

anything. So I decided on a sprint triathlon, complete with ocean swim!

I actually had to get a waiver for Parker because the age requirement was fifteen, and Parker was only twelve! When I explained to the race organizers what I was doing, they got on board and gave us permission. Crossing the finish line together will forever rank as one of my best memories, but the truth is, we bonded most during our training. Sometimes I pushed him, and sometimes he pushed me!

Men bond best when they break a sweat and break bread. My advice: train together, then eat together. It's a win-win all the way around. Pursuing a shared goal became a shared memory! And that triathlon prepared us for his Rite of Passage—hiking the Grand Canyon from rim to rim—which I'll detail in the next chapter.

The Mental Challenge

Until my senior year of college, I had read only half a dozen books *not* assigned by a teacher. And most of them were sports biographies with lots of stats and pictures. Then a flip switched during my senior year of college, and I fell in love with reading.

I once heard that the average author puts about two years of their life into every book they write. If that's true, reading one book is like gaining two years of life experience. As a young pastor, I lacked experience, so I had to borrow it from books. I averaged about two hundred books per year during those early years, which meant I gained four hundred years of life experience per year. So when someone asks me how old I am, I often answer in book age—I'm at least seven thousand years old.

Simply put, leaders are readers. And that's what I want my boys to be—not just gentlemen, but scholars. I want them to love learning. So I assigned a dozen books for them to read during their Year of Discipleship. What books? Well, several of the books were mine. I dedicated my first book, *In a Pit with a Lion on a Snowy Day*, to my three children, so why wouldn't I have them read it?

If you want to use some of my books, here are my top recommendations. *Soulprint* will help your son in the area of identity formation, which is mission critical at that age and stage. *The Circle Maker* will introduce your son to the practice of prayer. It also includes ten steps to setting life goals. You might even want to leverage *Draw the Circle* and do a forty-day prayer challenge with your son. Finally, I'd recommend ending your Year of Discipleship with *All In*—it's a Rite of Passage book that will challenge him to go all in with God.

I also have a few other suggestions related to genre and titles. Choose one or two biographies. Pick a missionary or a hero you think your son will identify with. Personally, I love Teddy Roosevelt. In fact, I've read at least five Roosevelt biographies. One word of advice—read the biography first to screen it for readability and excitability.

I assigned Dale Carnegie's *How to Win Friends and Influence People* simply because that's one of the books that made me fall in love with books. And I thought it would teach my sons some skill sets that will be incredibly useful their entire lives.

Depending on your son's personality, mix in some fiction titles. We read *The Alchemist* by Paulo Coelho. Coelho doesn't necessarily write from a Christian worldview, but the themes of the book made for great talking points.

I'd certainly mix in some books that will lay a foundation of faith, like *The Purpose Driven Life* by Rick Warren. Include some books that will stretch your son, like *Do Hard Things* by Alex and Brett Harris. And introduce your son to some of your favorite authors. Finally, add some fun-loving books, like Bob Goff's *Love Does*.

Remember, the goal isn't simply to read those books. It's to have twelve books about which you can have engaging conversation. Ultimately, you want to infect your son with a love of learning.

The Spiritual Challenge

The third and final challenge is spiritual. And let me say this up front: you can't lead someone where you haven't gone yourself. You have to *play the man* before you *make the man*. It doesn't mean you have to be perfect or we'd all be disqualified. The reality is, you'll grow through the Year of Discipleship as much as, or more than, your son. It's a wonderful win-win—it's as good for fathers as it is for sons.

The hands-down most important spiritual discipline is getting into God's Word on a daily basis. When you open the Bible, God opens His mouth. You can't get a word *from* God without getting into the Word *of* God. And the goal isn't getting through the Bible—it's getting the Bible through us. I certainly want my sons to grow up to be men of their word, but even more important, I want them to be men of the Word.

One footnote: my most prized possession is my grand-father's well-used 1934 *Thompson Chain-Reference Bible.* I love seeing the verses he underlined and the pages that are literally taped together because he turned to them so often. That family heirloom inspired me to follow suit—I want to read through enough Bibles that I can gift one to each of my children and, eventually, my grandchildren.

One habit I tried to inculcate in my kids during their Year of Discipleship was reading the Bible every day. Did we succeed in reading the Bible every day? No. But we were far more consistent than we would have been if we hadn't set the goal in the first place. And when you read the Bible in sync with your child, it inspires great conversations. During our Father-Son Meetings, we would often discuss what we were reading and learning.

Along with reading Scripture, I wanted to introduce my sons to some other spiritual disciplines. One way I did that is by leveraging Lent. Parker and I fasted from TV for forty days, which is no small accomplishment for a twelve-year-old kid. We also set our alarms for 6 a.m. on weekdays and knelt together in prayer. I wish I could tell you that it was pure revival every morning, but it wasn't. Some mornings our accomplishment was staying awake! But the experience was well worth it and will pay dividends for the rest of our lives. Plus, half the battle is just showing up. And that lesson isn't easily learned.

Finally, I challenged my sons to put together a life goal list. If you don't think that qualifies as spiritual, I beg to differ! I think it's the essence of faith. After all, faith is "being sure of what we hope for."[7] Parker started with twenty-five goals, some of which he adopted and adapted from my life goal list, making them shared goals. And we've accomplished several of them since then.

The goal of the discipleship process isn't just to make a man; it's to make a man of God. And that takes more than a father; it takes a spiritual father.

On that note, let me issue a challenge for those who don't have a biological father or a biological son. It doesn't mean you're the odd man out. Maybe there is someone you could ask to mentor you, and maybe there is someone you need to take under your wing.

Few people have had more influence in my life than my seventy-four-year-old friend and spiritual father, Dick Foth. He took me—a twenty-six-year-old pastor who didn't know which way was up—under his wing. I needed someone who had "been there, done that." Dick has not only walked me through pastoring and parenting, he's talked me off the ledge a few times. Without his influence in my life, I wouldn't be where I am today.

Dick and I didn't sign a Discipleship Covenant or do a Rite of Passage together. But we've had some shared experiences that have been nearly as bonding, including writing a book together—*A Trip around the Sun*. It might be worth adding to your reading list for the Discipleship Covenant.

One More Round

In the spirit of full disclosure, I think it's important for me to admit at this point that not everything went according to plan with either of my sons. There were even times when I wondered if it was a waste of time, but I refused to throw in the towel.

We didn't hit every target we shot at, but who bats a thousand?

Maybe you feel like you've tried and failed too many times. Remember Diana Nyad? Despite her repeated failures, she refused to give up on her dream. Quit beating yourself up over the mistakes you've made. You are not alone. And for the record, Aristotle Nyad may have crushed it on Diana's fifth birthday, but he fell short as a father, like the rest of us.

During Josiah's Year of Discipleship, I felt like I failed to live up to my end of the bargain. So much so that I asked for his forgiveness and a second chance. I got distracted by some of the demands and deadlines I was facing as a pastor and author. Josiah graciously forgave me, and we extended our timeline by sixth months. Then we failed to fulfill the physical challenge, which was to bike a century. Why? Because I had knee surgery! I'm still rehabbing that knee, and once it's ready, we're going to fulfill that challenge.

My point is that your plan won't go perfectly. You might even feel like it's not making a difference in your son's life. That's why you *sign* the covenant!

Don't give yourself an out.

"Fight one more round," said "Gentleman Jim" Corbett, the former heavyweight boxing champion of the world. "When your arms are so tired that you can hardly lift your hands to come on guard, fight one more round. When your nose is bleeding and your eyes are black and you are so tired that you wish your opponent would crack you one on the jaw and put you to sleep, fight one more round—remembering that the man who fights one more round is never whipped."[8]

You might lose a round or two, but keep coming out of your corner. You might have to restart the process a time or two. But even if you don't hit all of your goals, the effort will pay dividends the rest of your life and your son's life.

One last hard lesson learned. Since completing the Year of Discipleship with Parker, I feel like some of my intentionality has fallen off the radar. I wish we had maintained a Father-Son Meeting even after completing the covenant. No one can take the Year of Discipleship away from us, but I should have viewed it as a starting line, not the finish line.

As my kids get older, I have to keep growing as a parent. The challenges change, and so must I. One of my goals is to live to a hundred, which might take a miracle. If I make it, my children would be seventy-five, seventy-three, and sixty-eight respectively. But they would still be my children, and I would still be their father. Once a father, always a father!

Play the man!

Make the man!

10

The Rite of Passage

Show yourself a man.

—1 Kings 2:2 NASB

December 25, 1776
Trenton, New Jersey

In December 1776, the American Revolution seemed like a lost cause. After a demoralizing string of defeats, many members of General George Washington's army had deserted. Many more planned on leaving when their commission expired at year's end. The British were content retreating to their winter quarters to regroup and resupply for the spring campaign, but Washington had other plans.

A week before Christmas, Thomas Paine penned *The American Crisis*. It proved to be the right words at the right time—reviving the *esprit de corps* among the Continental army.

> These are the times that try men's souls. The summer soldier and the sunshine patriot will, in this crisis, shrink from the service of their country; but he that stands by it now, deserves the love and thanks of man and woman. Tyranny, like hell, is not easily conquered; yet we have this consolation with us, that the harder the conflict, the more glorious the triumph.[1]

With those words echoing in the soldiers' ears, Washington planned a daring offensive—daring because his army was vastly outnumbered and it would require crossing the half-frozen Delaware River after nightfall.

General Washington commandeered as many boats as he could find and commissioned watermen for a makeshift navy. Washington would attempt to cross three thousand infantry, plus canons. But he knew that if the enemy detected a single boat, the general and his entire army would be sitting ducks. That's what makes the crossing of the Delaware one of the most ingenious and courageous military maneuvers in American history. In fact, there might not be an America without it.

On Christmas morning, soldiers were issued three days' rations and fresh flints for their muskets. They were given orders to march as quietly as they could to McKonkey's Ferry. Washington planned on crossing shortly after sunset. What he didn't plan for was a brutal winter storm. Two soldiers would die of frostbite after the crossing, while the entire army left bloody footprints in the snow from severely frostbitten feet.[2] But that storm that "blew like a hurricane" proved to be a blessing in disguise. It gave Washington's army the cover it needed to cross in secrecy.

"Providence seemed to have smiled upon every part of this enterprise," said Henry Knox, General Washington's right-hand man.[3] In fact, Knox's account of the surprise attack likened it to the final battle scene in the book of Revelation. "Here succeeded a scene of war of which I had often conceived, but never saw before. The hurry, fright and confusion of the enemy was not unlike that which will be when the last trump shall sound."[4] Of course, the fact that the Hessian mercenaries were terribly hungover from Christmas festivities didn't hurt the cause either!

Only three Americans were killed, while Washington's army captured a thousand prisoners of war, plus their muskets, gunpowder, and artillery. It was a defining moment, a turning point in American history.

I'm not an art aficionado by any stretch, but I have a few favorites. The eight historic paintings that encircle the Capitol rotunda are spellbinding. Another favorite is the larger-than-life painting *Daniel in the Lions' Den* by Sir Peter Paul Rubens that hangs at the National Gallery of Art. And last but not least is Emanuel Gottlieb Leutze's 1851 painting, *Washington Crossing the Delaware*. When I first saw it hanging at the Metropolitan Museum of Art in New York City, it stopped me in my tracks!

Is the painting a romanticized version of what happened? Most definitely! In a more accurate portrayal, Washington would be obscured by snow, sleet, and hail, and there would be no shafts of light, because they crossed under the cover of a moonless night. But there is something so stirring, so symbolic, about Washington's stance—his face set like flint.[5]

He's a man on a mission, risking his very life for a cause he deemed worthy of dying for!

Not unlike Julius Caesar crossing the Rubicon River, it was a point of no return. It was do or die, all or nothing. There was no turning back! And in that sense, crossing the Delaware is a fitting metaphor for manhood.

Every man has a river to cross.

On one bank stands the boy, and the dangers of crossing the river are as real as the icy Delaware. But on the far shore stands a man—a man who beckons the boy to cross. It's a man who has been there, done that. It's the boy's father!

Crossing the Jordan

Just before crossing the Jordan River, Joshua issued a challenge to the Israelites. It's a timeless challenge, a promise with no expiration date.

> Consecrate yourselves, for tomorrow the LORD will do amazing things among you.[6]

We want to do amazing things for God, but that isn't our job. That's God's job! Our job is to consecrate ourselves! And if we do our job, God is going to show up and show off. He is the God who fights our battles for us, but we must consecrate ourselves to Him.

That's what the men of Israel did by literally circumcising themselves. It makes me grimace even thinking about it, but it reveals how seriously they took God's command. And it proved to be one of the most meaningful and memorable days of their lives. After all, you don't forget the day you cut off your foreskin. It was more than a physical act of consecration; it was a spiritual rite of passage.

It's the day God rolled away their reproach.

It's the day the men of Israel became men of God.

Then and only then were they ready to cross the river.

Our lives are marked by threshold moments—graduations, baptisms, weddings. Each entails one small step, one giant leap. But one threshold is mysteriously missing in our culture—the rite of passage to manhood.

In anthropology, the word *liminality* refers to a threshold moment in a person's life. It's often a ritual that changes someone's status, like a wedding. You're single one moment and married till death do you part the next. Or baptism—with one plunge you're dead to self and alive in Christ.

It's a new normal, a new chapter, a new creation.

It's a BC to AD moment.

We have liminal moments in our culture—securing a driver's license at sixteen, earning the right to vote at eighteen, and of course, being able to legally drink alcohol at twenty-one. But those are arbitrary and agnostic; they carry no spiritual significance.

We must give our sons a clear definition, a clear picture, of manhood. The seven virtues of manhood aren't a complete curriculum, but they are seven courses of action. We also owe our sons a rite of passage. Making a man cannot be reduced to a rite of passage any more than marriage can be reduced to a wedding. But that's where it starts.

"There is no place in our culture," said Robert Bly, "where boys are initiated consciously into manhood."[7] So what happens? We default to the cultural consensus—the voting age or legal drinking age.

We can do better; we must do better!

Otherwise we leave our sons in no man's land.

Defining Moment

Throughout history, different cultures have initiated their men in very different ways. A quick survey can provide some preliminary dos and don'ts.

In Jewish culture, a boy's rite of passage is called bar mitzvah. Historically, at thirteen years of age, a boy was fully accountable for his actions, which meant his father was no longer culpable for his son's sins. A boy was also given the rights and responsibilities of a man—the right to read from the Torah publically, the right to own property, and the right to get married. His manhood was symbolized with the tefillin, a small black box containing portions of the Torah that was worn like a headband or armband.

In Native American culture, the rite of passage is a vision quest that might involve a purification ceremony via a sweat lodge or a season spent alone in the wilderness.

For a medieval knight, the dubbing involved a ceremonial bath, fasting, an all-night prayer vigil, confession, Communion, and a sermon on the duties of a knight. Then, and only then, would the knight kneel at the altar so the priest could bless his sword.

The rite of passage for the young Masai warrior entailed killing a lion.

The Mandans go without food or drink or sleep for four days.

On Pentecost Island, members of the Naghol tribe climb a ninety-foot tower and then take a leap of faith with two vines attached around their ankles. The dive symbolizes a man's willingness to sacrifice his life for his tribe.

Then there's the Brazilian Sateré-Mawé tradition of a boy putting on gloves filled with bullet ants. According to the Schmidt Sting Pain Index, the bullet ant has the most painful sting of any insect in the world. A single sting is comparable to being shot with a bullet, hence the name! A boy must endure the stings for ten minutes without screaming or showing signs of weakness. The pain lasts a full twenty-four hours, but the boy is one step closer to becoming a man. Once he completes this ritual twenty times, it's official.[8]

Some of these rites of passage seem rather archaic or downright wrong. And I'm not advocating anything that entails cruel and unusual punishment. But a man needs a test, a trial. That's how we prove our manhood. I'm certainly not going to put gloves filled with bullet ants on my sons' hands, but I'm not going to treat them with kid gloves either.

Forgive the rabbit trail, but if every kid gets a trophy, how will they learn to deal with the agony of defeat or overcome the fear of failure? When we treat boys like boys, they remain boys! Like a caterpillar that can't grow wings without fighting its way out of the cocoon, a boy needs to fight for his manhood.

A rite of passage doesn't have to be life threatening, but I'd recommend a well-planned and well-controlled element of danger and adventure. That's what I tried to do with both of my sons and my daughter.

Take, for example, the five-day rafting trip down the Colorado River I took with Josiah. Is it any coincidence that the most memorable moments from that trip doubled as the most dangerous? It was surviving the class 7 rapids that could have capsized our raft; it was climbing cliffs that scared the heck out of us; it was coming within a foot of a rattlesnake while hiking out of the canyon. There is something about death-defying adventure that is life-giving!

I've already shared the story, but the truly liminal moment for Josiah was mile marker 79.1 on the Colorado River. The journey from boyhood to manhood is a process, but the threshold was Sockdolager. He was a boy on the near side, a man on the far side. That's where Josiah crossed the river of manhood—literally and figuratively.

Parker's Rite of Passage was a 23.2-mile rim-to-rim hike that entailed a one-mile elevation descent down the North Kaibab Trail and a one-mile elevation ascent up the Bright Angel Trail. The toughest thing about it was that we did this trek when temperatures hit 110 degrees in the shade. I lost thirteen pounds in two days! At one point I thought we might have to get helicoptered out. It's impossible to stay hydrated in those temperatures, and we ran out of water with four miles of trail left. I kept asking Parker, "On a scale of one to ten, how are you?" When Parker said, "Negative one," I got scared for him—and for me. If I didn't get Parker out of that canyon alive, I wasn't sure I would have a home to go back to!

When we finally reached the South Rim of the canyon and looked back at the trail we had traversed, it was a liminal moment. A boy entered the canyon, but a young man emerged.

The Rite of Passage is more than a formality, more than a frivolity. It's a defining moment. I planned an adventure to mark that moment, but that's not all. I also planned a ceremony.

The Ceremony

"Men are God's method," writes E. M. Bounds. "The Church is looking for better methods; God is looking for better men."[9]

I couldn't agree more, but we need a method to make a man too. In fact, that's what's missing. At the end of our Year of Discipleship, I knew I wanted to go on a pilgrimage of sorts with my sons. And we did. But just as important as the pilgrimage was the Rite of Passage ceremony.

I've already detailed the plan I pulled off with Parker, staging a rather elaborate surprise at Roosevelt Island. I did the same with Josiah. In both instances, their uncles had a prepared speech, a symbolic gift, and a keepsake letter. When each boy stood in front of the Youth Stone and Manhood Stone, it marked another liminal moment.

One of the most important aspects of the Rite of Passage is writing a letter to your son—a letter that will hopefully become a keystone and perhaps even a keepsake. The letters I wrote to my sons are so personal, so sacred that I won't share them. But I will offer a few tips that should help you get started.

First, speak words of affirmation. Call out the character traits and spiritual gifts you see in him. Tell him you're in his corner no matter what. Reassure him that your love isn't performance-based. And remind him that he's divinely unique and doesn't need to be anyone other than the person God created him to be!

Second, issue a challenge. Exhort him to go after God with all of his heart. Of course, you need to set the standard by leading the way. Give your son biblical promises to stand on. Remind him of your core values. And reassure him of God's plans and purposes for his life.

Third, keep it real. While you want to speak faith into your son's future, don't forget to admit your own shortcomings. That relieves the pressure of having to be perfect. It also lays the foundation for a more authentic relationship. And don't forget to share some of the lessons you learned at his age, lessons you learned the hard way!

The goal of the letter is to give your son written proof of your love—it's a written blessing. But I also wanted each of my sons to have more than a special memory of their Rite of Passage, which tends to fade with time. So I gave them symbolic gifts to mark the moment.

Josiah received a nice lighter that symbolizes Paul's exhortation to Timothy in 2 Timothy 1:6: "Fan into flame the gift of God." I also gave him a carved elephant that his grandfather got on his first mission trip to Africa. I leveraged that elephant by challenging Josiah to live up to the legacy of his namesake. Finally, I gave him his first razor, which he didn't need just yet. I wanted that razor to remind him of 1 Timothy 4:12: "Don't let anyone look down on you because you are young, but set an example for the believers in speech, in conduct, in love, in faith and in purity." In their own unique way, each of those gifts is a tangible reminder to play the man.

After giving my sons their letters and gifts, our entourage headed to the nearest Ruth's Chris Steak House! We topped off each of my sons' ceremonies with a filet mignon cooked to perfection and served on a five-hundred-degree plate with extra butter sauce. That first bite of steak is another liminal moment!

There you have it—the nuts and bolts. But if you visit www.playtheman.com, you'll find additional resources and free downloads.

Rim Huggers

Of all the life goals I've achieved, rafting the Colorado River with Josiah and hiking the Grand Canyon with Parker rank right at the top.

Rafting the river.

Crossing the canyon.

Same difference!

As Parker and I hiked our way out of the canyon, zigzagging up the final stretch of Bright Angel Trail, we spotted hundreds of sightseers lining the South Rim. Maybe it was the exhaustion from two days of hiking, but I had a moment of revelation. Our clothes were caked with orange-colored canyon clay mixed with salty sweat stains. Flies hovered. We were parched and scorched, bone-weary. And there stood these sightseers, looking like they had just emerged from their air-conditioned hotel rooms after a cool shower, zestfully clean. Some of them were even licking ice cream cones!

For a split second, I hated those sightseers! Then I felt sorry for them. They were *seeing it* and *missing it* at the same time. Why? Because you cannot fully appreciated what you have not personally experienced. That's when I came up with a name for the people who stay at a distance, standing and staring, but never hiking into the canyon—rim huggers![10]

It reminds me of "The Man in the Arena," an epic speech by Teddy Roosevelt.

It is not the critic who counts; not the man who points out how the strong man stumbles, or where the doer of deeds could have done them better. The credit belongs to the man who is actually in the arena, whose face is marred by dust and sweat and blood; who strives valiantly; who errs, who comes short again and again, because there is no effort without error and shortcoming; but who does actually strive to do the deeds; who knows great enthusiasms, the great devotions; who spends himself in a worthy cause; who at the best knows in the end the triumph of high achievement, and who at the worst, if he fails, at least fails while daring greatly, so that his place shall never be with those cold and timid souls who neither know victory nor defeat.[11]

Churches are filled with rim huggers who feel like they've done their religious duty by sitting in a pew for sixty minutes. Listen, you cannot be the hands and feet of Jesus if you're sitting on your butt. Church is not a spectator sport. And neither is fatherhood.

Playing the man is the hardest thing you'll ever do. A close second is making the man. But that's what makes it noble. It takes tough love, childlike wonder, will power, raw passion, true grit, clear vision, and moral courage. At points you'll wonder if you'll ever make it. Those are the moments when you must strive valiantly and dare greatly as a father. If you do, you'll make a man.

We want joy without sacrifice.

We want character without suffering.

We want success without failure.

We want gain without pain.

We want a testimony without the test.

We want it all, without going all in.

It doesn't work that way, and you know it. You don't get credit for an audit. You'll get out of fatherhood what you put into it. Will you make mistakes? More than you can count.

Will your sons turn out to be perfect? Probably as perfect as you. But may you have the same resolve as Joshua, who led the men of Israel across the Jordan.

As for me and my household, we will serve the LORD.[12]

The Blessing

When everything is said and done, I hope my children grow up to love God and love their parents. Of course, I cannot control either outcome. But I need to be able to look in the mirror and know that I gave them my very best effort. I want them to know one thing beyond a shadow of a doubt—they are my beloved sons, my beloved daughter, in whom I am well pleased.[13]

That's *the* blessing!

The Father pronounced that blessing when Jesus was baptized. And while we read right past it, Jesus never forgot it. That blessing echoed in His ears forever.

This might sound sacrilegious, but it could be argued that Jesus had underachieved at thirty years of age. He had unparalleled power, unmatched wisdom, yet all He had to show for it was some tables and chairs He had made in His earthly father's carpenter shop. Jesus hadn't performed any miracles or told any parables at this point. So from a human perspective, wouldn't you wonder if His Father was a wee bit disappointed? But the heavenly Father doesn't love us based on who we are; He loves us based on who He is. His love is not based on our performance; it's based on His character. God is love!

I've challenged you to play the man and make the man, but these aren't accomplished via human effort. They're not things you *do* for God; God *does* them for you. You are the man, in Christ.

We don't find our identity in what we have done for God. We find our identity in what Christ has done for us.

I'll fall short a thousand times as a father, but I pray that my children have a Matthew 3:17 moment. I want them to hear, loud and clear, that they are beloved. I want them to know that I am well pleased. Not because of what they've done, for better or for worse, but because of who they are—my son, my daughter.

My sons may not remember their Rite of Passage the way I do. In fact, I'm sure they won't. But I hope the spirit behind all of my efforts echoes in their ears for all eternity—*you are my beloved son, in whom I am well pleased.*

When you fail as an earthly father, remember that the heavenly Father more than compensates for your mistakes! If you're a single dad, it might take twice the effort to disciple your son. But you aren't alone; you and God are a divine tag team. As an earthly father, I want to be the best reflection of the heavenly Father possible. But I'm just a man trying to make a man. There is a man—the Son of Man, the Son of God—who won the battle for us. And we follow in His footsteps.

Play the man!

EPILOGUE

Be on the alert, stand firm in the faith, act like men, be strong.

—1 Corinthians 16:13 NASB

October 16, 1555
Oxford, England

They would become known as the three Oxford Martyrs of Anglicanism—Bishops Hugh Latimer, Nicholas Ridley, and Thomas Cranmer. Like Polycarp twelve centuries before, they would not recant their convictions.

Hugh Latimer was a prince of preachers, appointed university preacher of prestigious Cambridge University. He also served as the personal chaplain to King Edward VI. Nicholas Ridley was the bishop of London and Westminster and, like Latimer, served as one of the king's chaplains. Thomas Cranmer held the highest office in the Church of England, archbishop of Canterbury. Cranmer was a leader of the English Reformation and, with Ridley's help, composed *The Book of Common Prayer*.

When the Catholic Queen Mary, known as "Bloody Mary," took the throne of England in 1553, their positions of power and pulpits of authority were put in jeopardy. Would they compromise their convictions to pacify the queen, or would they continue to preach their convictions to please the King? Latimer, Ridley, and Cranmer could have compromised, could have escaped, but instead they stayed and played the man to the bitter end.

During their unjust imprisonment, they prayed with the passion of Shadrach, Meshach, and Abednego—not for their escape but for the restoration of the gospel in England.

On October 16, 1555, the three bishops were led outside the city gate and fastened to a stake. When the first log was lit beneath Ridley's feet, Latimer uttered the very same words that Polycarp had heard from heaven twelve centuries earlier:

Be of good comfort, Master Ridley, and play the man. We shall this day light such a candle, by God's grace, in England, as I trust shall never be put out.[1]

When you *play the man*, when you *make the man* you are lighting a candle for the next generation—a candle that shall never be put out.

Play the man!

Make the man!

NOTES

Introduction

1. Leonard L. Thompson, "The Martyrdom of Polycarp," *The Journal of Religion* 82, no. 1 (January 2002): 27; Polycarp's date of death is the subject of much debate. It cannot be determined authoritatively, but I've chosen the date that best fits the facts based on scholarly opinion and my own personal research.

2. Kenneth Howell, *Ignatius of Antioch and Polycarp of Smyrna* (Zanesville, OH: CHResources, 2009), 168–69.

3. Ibid., 169.

4. "The Indian School at William and Mary," William and Mary, accessed September 1, 2016, http://www.wm.edu/about/history/historiccampus/indian school/index.php.

5. Andrew Carroll, *Letters of a Nation* (New York: Broadway Books, 1999), 238.

6. Matthew 10:16.

7. George Monbiot, "For More Wonder, Rewild the World," TED talk, filmed July 2013, 3:00, https://www.ted.com/talks/george_monbiot_for_more_wonder _rewild_the_world/transcript?language=en.

8. See Matthew 7:15.

9. Matthew 8:20.

10. It's also the title of a book by Dr. John Gray.

11. Genesis 1:27.

12. David Brooks, *The Road to Character* (New York: Random House, 2015), xi.

13. "James A. Garfield," *Wikiquote*, accessed October 19, 2016, https://en.wiki quote.org/wiki/James_A._Garfield.

Chapter 1 Tough as Nails

1. "Home," Charles Lindbergh, accessed September 2, 2016, http://www .charleslindbergh.com/history/paris.asp.

2. Bill Bryson, *One Summer* (New York: Doubleday, 1912), 40.

3. Ibid., 40.

4. "Medical Aspects of the Crucifixion of Christ," accessed September 2, 2016, http://www.frugalsites.net/jesus/medical.html.

5. Ibid.

6. See Romans 5:7–8.

7. See 1 Corinthians 13:7.

8. "Thomas Becket," Wikipedia, accessed September 2, 2016, https://en.wiki pedia.org/wiki/Thomas_Becket.

9. "Thomas Becket," Marianne Dorman's Catholic Website, accessed September 2, 2016, http://mariannedorman.homestead.com/Becket.html.

10. Justin Welby, speech, March 2, 2016, New Wine Conference, Harrogate, England.

11. *Rocky III*. Directed by Sylvester Stalone. Hollywood, CA: United Artists, 1982.

12. Emma Young, "Do Get Mad: The Upside of Anger," *New Scientist*, February 6, 2013, https://www.newscientist.com/article/mg21729032-700-do-get-mad -the-upside-of-anger/.

13. See Romans 12:9.

14. *The Third Man*. Directed by Carol Reed. London: London Films, 1949.

15. Ecclesiastes 12:11.

16. See Ephesians 4:15.

17. "Toughskins," *Wikipedia*, accessed September 5, 2016, https://en.wikipedia .org/wiki/Toughskins.

18. In case you care, it was *The Circle Maker*.

19. I first heard this idea from Erwin McManus. So good. So true.

20. Mark 15:13.

21. Luke 23:34.

22. John 11:35.

Chapter 2 A Gentleman and a Scholar

1. Henry Blodgett, "Here's the Famous Populist Speech Teddy Roosevelt Gave Right after Getting Shot," *Business Insider*, October 14, 2011, http://www .businessinsider.com/heres-the-famous-populist-speech-teddy-roosevelt-gave -right-after-getting-shot-2011-10.

2. Brett and Kate McKay, "Lessons in Manliness: Theodore Roosevelt on Living the Strenuous Life," The Art of Manliness, February 21, 2008, http://www .artofmanliness.com/2008/02/21/lessons-in-manliness-theodore-roosevelt-on -living-the-strenuous-life/.

3. Edmund Morris, *The Rise of Theodore Roosevelt* (New York: Random House, 2010), xxiv.

4. Ibid.

5. Thanks to Ashley Montagu for this phrase!

6. Paul Reber, "What Is the Memory Capacity of the Human Brain?" *Scientific American*, May 1, 2010, https://www.scientificamerican.com/article/what-is-the -memory-capacity/.

7. "Human Brain – Neuroscience – Cognitive Science," Basic Knowledge 101, accessed October 19, 2016, http://www.basicknowledge101.com/subjects/brain.html.

8. A. J. Jacobs, "The Know-It-All: One Man's Humble Quest to Become the Smartest Person in the World" (New York: Simon and Schuster, 2004), 2.

9. "Mahatma Gandhi," Good Reads, accessed October 19, 2016, https://www.goodreads.com/quotes/2253-live-as-if-you-were-to-die-tomorrow-learn-as.

10. Kathryn Zickhur and Lee Rainie, "A Snapshot of Reading in America in 2013," Pew Research Center, January 16, 2014, http://www.pewinternet.org/2014/01/16/a-snapshot-of-reading-in-america-in-2013/.

11. Edward Iwata, "Naisbatt Turns Lust for Life into Mega Book Career," *USA Today*, September 25, 2006, http://usatoday30.usatoday.com/money/books/2006-09-24-naisbitt-usat_x.htm.

12. J. D. Salinger, *Catcher in the Rye* (Boston: Little, Brown, 1991), 62.

13. He recently retired the title. Guys, this is your chance.

14. *Merriam-Webster Online*, s.v. "Gentleman," http://www.merriam-webster.com/dictionary/gentleman.

15. See John 8:1–11.

16. See Luke 7:37-50.

17. John 19:27.

18. See Galatians 5:22–23 for a list of the fruit of the Spirit.

19. Dallas Willard, *The Divine Conspiracy: Rediscovering Our Hidden Life in God* (San Francisco: HarperSanFrancisco, 1998), 94.

20. Albert Einstein, "Religion and Science," *New York Times Magazine*, November 9, 1930.

21. 1 Kings 4:29, 32–33.

22. Proverbs 25:2.

23. Francis Bacon, *The Works of Francis Bacon*, ed. Basil Montagu (Philadelphia: Hart, 1852), 176.

24. Al Seckle, "Visual Illusions That Show How We (Mis)think," TED, February 2004, https://www.ted.com/talks/al_seckel_says_our_brains_are_mis_wired/transcript?language=en.

25. Richard Restak, *Mozart's Brain and the Fighter Pilot: Unleashing Your Brain's Potential* (New York: Harmony, 2001), 92.

26. John 4:22.

27. John 4:24.

28. 2 Timothy 2:15 KJV 2000.

29. See Deuteronomy 17:18–19.

30. Every year I try to pick a plan from the dozens of plans on the YouVersion app. I'd highly recommend shopping for a plan that will fit your rhythm of life but also stretch you spiritually.

31. 2 Timothy 4:13.

32. Doug Batchelor, "The Beginning of Wisdom," LightSource, accessed September 6, 2016, http://www.lightsource.com/ministry/amazing-facts/articles/the-beginning-of-wisdom-14923.html.

33. See Genesis 15:5.

34. Proverbs 27:17.

35. "The Strenuous Life," *Wikipedia*, accessed October 19, 20016, https://en.wikipedia.org/wiki/The_Strenuous_Life.

36. Mark Batterson, *In a Pit with a Lion on a Snowy Day: How to Survive and Thrive When Opportunity Roars* (Colorado Springs: Multnomah, 2016), 159.

37. 1 Corinthians 13:11.

38. Robert Sapolsky, "Dude, Where's My Frontal Cortex?" *Nautilus*, July 24, 2014, http://nautil.us/issue/15/turbulence/dude-wheres-my-frontal-cortex.

39. Arthur Gordon, *Wonder* (Grand Rapids: Revell, 2006), 182.

40. Ibid., 182.

41. "Now We Are Small Enough," Bible.org, accessed October 19, 2016, https://bible.org/illustration/now-we-are-small-enough.

42. Sir Arthur Conan Doyle, *The Sign of the Four* (North Charleston, SC: CreateSpace Independent Publishing Platform, 2016), 49.

Chapter 3 Unbroken

1. Laura Hillenbrand, *Unbroken* (New York: Random House, 2010), 173.

2. Viktor Frankl, *Man's Search for Meaning* (Boston: Beacon Press, 2006).

3. John 16:33.

4. George Bernard Shaw, *Mrs. Warren's Confessions* (Seaside, OR: Watchmaker Publishing, 2010), 49.

5. Daniel Goleman, *Emotional Intelligence* (New York: Bantam, 2005), 80–83.

6. Ibid., 81–82.

7. 1 Corinthians 10:23 BSB.

8. Matthew 16:10.

9. Luke 4:4.

10. Matthew 26:53.

11. Hebrews 4:15.

12. 2 Samuel 11:1–3.

13. Luke 4:1–2.

14. Luke 4:4.

15. Deuteronomy 24:5.

16. Matthew 5:29–30.

17. 1 Corinthians 10:13.

18. 1 Samuel 24:3–4.

19. Craig Lambert, "'Bobby' Jones," *Harvard Magazine*, March–April 2002, http://harvardmagazine.com/2002/03/bobby-jones.html.

20. See 1 Samuel 24:5.

Chapter 4 The Three-Headed Dragon

1. Lee Stetson, *The Wild Muir* (Berkeley: Heyday, 1994), ix.

2. For a complete list of my 115 life goals, check out *The Circle Maker*.

3. "Why John Muir," The John Muir Way, accessed October 27, 2016, http://johnmuirway.org/why-john-muir.

4. "John Muir," *Wikipedia*, accessed September 8, 2016, https://en.wikipedia.org/wiki/John_Muir.

5. Stetson, *The Wild Muir*, 21.

6. Ibid., 109–10.

7. Mark 1:8.

8. Luci Shaw, *Water My Soul* (Vancouver: Regent College Publishing, 1998), 10.

9. Matthew 8:20.

10. John 2:17.

11. Dorothy L. Sayer, "The Greatest Drama Ever Staged," in *Letters to a Diminished Church: Passionate Arguments for the Relevance of Christian Doctrine* (Nashville: W Publishing Group, 2004), 4.

12. C. S. Lewis, *Weight of Glory* (Grand Rapids: Zondervan, 2001), 26.

13. Revelation 12:4.

14. See 1 John 4:4.

15. Genesis 3:1.

16. New Wine Conference, Harrogate, UK, March 2, 2016.

17. Genesis 3:6.

18. Edmund Burke, "Thoughts on the Cause of the Present Discontents," in *Select Works of Edmund Burke*, vol. 1 (Indianapolis, IN: Liberty Fund, 1999), 146.

19. Genesis 3:12.

20. C. S. Lewis, *Mere Christianity* (New York: HarperOne, 1980), 136.

21. Genesis 3:5.

22. "Tree Facts," North Carolina State University, accessed September 9, 2016, https://www.ncsu.edu/project/treesofstrength/treefact.htm.

23. "Hedonic treadmill," Wikipedia, accessed September 9, 2016, https://en.wikipedia.org/wiki/Hedonic_treadmill.

24. Ephesians 5:25.

25. Genesis 3:10.

Chapter 5 Sockdolager

1. Edward Dolnick, *Down the Great Unknown* (New York: HarperCollins, 2001), 14.

2. Ibid., 19.

3. Ibid.

4. A. W. Tozer, *Culture* (Chicago: Moody, 2016), 28.

5. The rapids on this run were graded from 1 to 10.

6. *Wiktionary, The Free Dictionary*, s.v. "sockdolager," accessed December 19, 2016, https://en.wiktionary.org/wiki/sockdolager.

7. Friedrich Nietzsche, *The Anti-Christ, Ecce Homo, Twilight of the Idols, and Other Writings*, ed. Aaron Ridley and Judith Norman, trans. Judith Norman (Cambridge, United Kingdom: Cambridge University Press, 2005), 157.

8. Kelly Clarkson, "Stronger (What Doesn't Kill You)," in *Stronger*, RCA Records, 2011.

9. Genesis 1:28.

10. Dolnick, *Great Unknown*, 19.

11. "Earth," *Wikipedia*, accessed October 19, 2016, https://en.wikipedia.org/wiki/Earth.

12. Robert Frost, "The Road Not Taken," accessed September 28, 2016, http://www.poetryfoundation.org/poem/173536.

13. Romans 8:37.

14. See Proverbs 16:32.

15. David Brooks, *The Road to Character* (New York: Random House, 2015), 52.

16. Ibid., 52.

17. Ibid., 60.

18. See 2 Corinthians 10:5.

19. See Job 31:1.

20. See Luke 9:23.

21. See 1 Corinthians 9:27.

22. See Galatians 5:24.

23. Brooks, *Road to Character*, 61.

24. Revelation 2:20.

25. See James 3:3–6.

26. Ephesians 5:4.

27. Jeremiah 1:7 KJV.

28. James 3:3–6.

29. I highly recommend Angela Duckworth's book, *Grit*. This definition is a derivation of her work.

30. Gordon MacDonald, *A Resilient Life* (Nashville: Thomas Nelson, 2009), vii.

31. See Genesis 32:22–32.

32. Luke 22:44.

33. Hebrews 12:2.

34. Hebrews 12:1–2.

35. "Roger Bannister," *Wikipedia*, accessed September 12, 2016, https://en.wikipedia.org/wiki/Roger_Bannister.

36. See 1 Samuel 14.

37. Dolnick, *Great Unknown*, 71.

38. Ibid., 85.

39. "John Wesley Powell," *Wikipedia*, accessed September 12, 2016, https://en.wikipedia.org/wiki/John_Wesley_Powell.

40. Dolnick, *Great Unknown*, 89.

Chapter 6 Born for the Storm

1. Jon Meacham, *American Lion* (New York: Random House, 2008), 29.

2. Ibid., vii.

3. Luke 4:18–19.

4. Luke 4:21.

5. Meacham, *American Lion*, 14.

6. "Advice to Andrew Jackson by His Mother," Valley Station Church of Christ, accessed September 13, 2016, http://www.vscoc.org/Bulletinfdr/advice_to_andrew_jackson.htm.

7. Genesis 2:18.

8. "Advice to Andrew Jackson by His Mother," Valley Station Church of Christ.

9. Meacham, *American Lion*, 19.

10. Ibid.

11. 1 Corinthians 16:13 AKJV.

12. 1 Samuel 30:6 ESV.

13. *The Blues Brothers*. Directed by John Landis. Universal City, CA: Universal Pictures, 1980.

14. Matthew 11:12 NASB.

15. Matthew 3:17 ESV.

16. 1 Samuel 14:35.

17. 1 Samuel 15:12 NLT.

Chapter 7 Call of Duty

1. "Attempted Assassination of Ronald Reagan," *Wikipedia*, accessed September 12, 2016, https://en.wikipedia.org/wiki/Attempted_assassination_of_Ronald_Reagan.

2. Romans 5:6–8.

3. C. S. Lewis, *The Screwtape Letters* (New York: HarperCollins, 1996), 161.

4. C. S. Lewis, *The Complete C. S. Lewis Signature Classics* (New York: Harper One, 2007), 270.

5. Mark 15:15.

6. Martin Luther King Jr., "Letter from Birmingham Jail," The King Center, accessed December 19, 2016, www.thekingcenter.org/archive/document/letter-birmingham-city-jail-0.

7. Ibid.

8. Ella Wheeler Wilcox, "Protest," in *Poems of Problems* (Chicago: W. B. Conkey Company, 1914), 154, https://archive.org/details/poemsproblems00wilcrich.

9. If you want to explore this idea, watch the TED video by Mellody Hopson, "Color Blind or Color Brave?" filmed March 2014, https://www.ted.com/talks/mellody_hobson_color_blind_or_color_brave?language=en.

10. 1 Samuel 24:5.

11. Proverbs 22:6.

12. Roland Herbert Bainton, *Here I Stand: A Life of Martin Luther* (Peabody, MA: Hendrickson, 2009), 180.

13. "Sing Out, Mr. President: Andrew Jackson's One-Man Majority," NPR.org, February 20, 2011, http://www.npr.org/sections/deceptivecadence/2011/02/21/133843232/sing-out-mr-president-andrew-jacksons-one-man-majority.

14. Romans 12:2.

15. See Romans 1:16.

16. Acts 4:13.

17. 2 Timothy 1:7.

18. Penn Jillette, "Penn Jillette on Sharing Your Faith," Vimeo video, posted November 6, 2012, https://vimeo.com/52957285.

19. Matthew 28:19.

20. Annie Dillard, *Teaching a Stone to Talk* (New York: Harper Perennial, 2013), 52.

21. Mark Batterson, *Wild Good Chase: Reclaim the Adventure of Pursuing God* (Colorado Springs: Multnomah, 2008), 150.

22. Matthew 16:18.

23. Isaiah 9:6–7.

Chapter 8 No Man's Land

1. Robert A. Caro, *The Path to Power: The Years of Lyndon Johnson* (New York: Vintage Books, 1990), 309.

2. Ibid.

3. This may be an ancient overstatement. Modern revisions posit a much smaller number. But either way, the Spartans were vastly outnumbered, even with the help of several other Greek city-states.

4. Helena P. Schrader, *Leonidas of Sparta: A Heroic King* (Tucson: Wheatmark, 2012), 518.

5. "The Battle of Thermopylae," Sam Houston State University, accessed October 25, 2016, http://www.shsu.edu/~his_ncp/Herother.html.

6. Malachi 4:6 KJV.

7. Andy Stanley, *Choosing to Cheat* (Colorado Springs: Multnomah, 2003), 10.

8. Lyle W. Dorsett, *A Passion for God: The Spiritual Journey of A. W. Tozer* (Chicago: Moody, 2008), 160.

9. "Ship Statistics and Details," The *Queen Mary*, accessed September 15, 2016, http://www.queenmary.com/history/comparison-fun-facts/facts-statistics/.

10. Luke 1:15–17.

11. *Braveheart*, directed by Mel Gibson (Los Angeles: Icon Productions, 1995).

Chapter 9 The Discipleship Covenant

1. Diana Nyad, *Find a Way* (New York: Alfred A. Knopf, 2015), 15.

2. Diana Nyad, "Never, Ever Give Up," TEDWomen, December 2013, https://www.ted.com/talks/diana_nyad_never_ever_give_up/transcript?language=en.

3. Nyad, *Find a Way*, 4.

4. Ibid., 27–28.

5. Ibid., 28.

6. Proverbs 18:21.

7. Hebrews 11:1 NET.

8. Brett and Kate McKay, *Art of Manliness* (Cincinnati: How Books, 2011), 147.

Chapter 10 The Rite of Passage

1. "The American Crisis," *Wikipedia*, accessed October 25, 2016, https://en.wikipedia.org/wiki/The_American_Crisis.

2. Jane Hampton Cook, *Battlefield & Blessings* (Chattanooga: God and Country Press, 2007), 237.

3. Ibid., 245.

4. Ibid., 239.

5. See Isaiah 50:7.

6. Joshua 3:5.

7. Robert Bly with Bill Moyer, "A Gathering of Men," PBS, January 8, 1990, www.pbs.org/moyers/journal/archives/gathering.html.

8. "Ten Incredibly Painful Rites of Initiation," List Verse, July 17, 2010, http://listverse.com/2010/07/17/10-incredibly-painful-rites-of-initiation/.

9. E. M. Bounds, *Power through Prayer* (Seaside, OR: Rough Draft Printing, 2013), 5.

10. Mark Batterson, *All In: You Are One Decision Away from a Totally Different Life* (Grand Rapids: Zondervan, 2015), 76.

11. President Theodore Roosevelt, "Citizenship in a Republic" (speech), the Sorbonne, Paris, France, April 23, 1910, http://www.theodore-roosevelt.com/tr sorbonnespeech.html.

12. Joshua 24:15.

13. See Matthew 3:17.

Epilogue

1. William Byron Forbush, *Fox's Book of Martyrs* (Grand Rapids: Zondervan), 237.

Mark Batterson is the *New York Times* bestselling author of *The Circle Maker*, *The Grave Robber*, *A Trip around the Sun*, and *If*. He is the lead pastor of National Community Church, one church with eight campuses in Washington, DC. Mark has a doctor of ministry degree from Regent University and lives on Capitol Hill with his wife, Lora, and their three children. Learn more at www.markbatterson.com.

Discover resources for individuals and small groups at

MARKBATTERSON.COM

You will find . . .

Sermon outlines

Church resources

Printable bookmark, flyer, and more